Betty Crocker's
30-MINUTE MENUS

Betty Crocker's
30-MINUTE
MENUS

PRENTICE HALL

NEW YORK   LONDON   TORONTO   SYDNEY   TOKYO   SINGAPORE

PRENTICE HALL GENERAL REFERENCE
15 Columbus Circle
New York, NY 10023

Library of Congress Cataloging-in-Publication Data

Betty Crocker's 30-minute menus.
     p.   cm.
   Includes index.
   ISBN 0-13-085192-2
    1. Quick and easy cookery. 2. Menus. I. Prentice Hall, inc.
  II. Title: Betty Crocker's thirty-minute menus.
  TX833.5.B48 1992
  641.5'55—dc20   91-15714
                                     CIP

Manufactured in the United States of America

10 9 8 7 6 5 4 3 2 1

First Edition

Cover: Menu #18 (page 56)

Frontis: Menu #32 (page 91)

CONTENTS

INTRODUCTION
vii

Menu #70 (page 199)

INTRODUCTION

Everyone is extremely busy these days and looking for ways to save time without getting shortchanged on quality. With *30-Minute Menus* you'll find both speed and quality, and see that it *is* possible to still cook delicious, homemade meals for family and friends. We promise you'll have dinner on the table in half-hour, or less!

You have asked us again and again for meals that can be made quickly, and we are glad to oblige with this book, as these are the meals we often need ourselves. With dual-career families on the rise, and the more complex schedules of the average family, it is harder and harder to get everyone together for dinner, much less find the time to cook it! *30-Minute Menus* is our solution to the problem of time management, one that absolutely doesn't skimp on taste or creativity.

We turned to our test kitchens to create complete menus, testing each combination of recipes thoroughly to ensure taste, ease and speed. You can count on these menus to satisfy all your cooking requirements, from an elegant meal of Avocado-Crab Soup with Cheddar-Corn Muffins and a fresh tossed salad, to hearty picnic fare of Quick Barbecued Chicken Wings, Potato-Corn Salad, Bread and Butter Pickles and Lemonade Tea.

In the first chapter we've gathered tips to help streamline your kitchen and stock your pantry efficiently. You'll also find loads of ideas on how to jazz up store-bought products, turn leftovers into another terrific dish and dovetail cooking to net faster meals as well as leftovers to form the basis of another dinner.

You'll also learn how to use these menus easily. Each has an overall list of ingredients for the entire menu to make marketing a snap, a special menu tip and a timetable to simplify meal preparation further. All the menus serve four comfortably, and come with calorie counts and nutrition information. While not a diet book, all the menus are well balanced, and we have been careful in using salt, sugar and fat.

We know you'll find *30-Minute Menus* a welcome addition to your busy life. Sitting down with family and friends for a relaxing, home-cooked meal at the end of the day doesn't have to be a wistful memory; it can be a daily reality. We've gathered all the information, tips and great recipes you'll need right here—the only thing missing is hours in the kitchen!

THE BETTY CROCKER EDITORS

CHAPTER 1
SOLVING THE
TIME CRUNCH

This book assures you delicious, innovative and well-balanced meals in about the same time you spend watching the evening news. You may have thought that preparing real, home-cooked meals for family and friends wasn't possible on an average day. However, satisfying dinners don't have to take a great deal of time when you follow the suggestions, tips and organizational advice we've gathered here.

MENU TIPS

♦ All the menus in this book have been tested in our Betty Crocker Kitchens, and from the first step to the moment you serve dinner, each menu takes only thirty minutes—or less. However, we do recommend that you read through the recipes and the timetable thoroughly before starting your countdown; stopping to backtrack or clarify will add extra time to your schedule.

♦ Each menu comes with a list of every ingredient you'll need to prepare the meal. Be sure to check the list and jot down any necessary items on your shopping list.

♦ These aren't diet menus, of course, but we have been careful in using salt, sugar and fat, as well as to offer a variety of main-dish choices that vary from meat to fish to vegetarian. Every menu is a complete meal, whether a light one of sandwiches and fruit or heartier fare complete with dessert. You'll also find a complete chapter of menus for the microwave to make the best use of this terrific timesaver.

How to Read the Menus

♦ Every menu begins with the list of recipes for that meal. Every item with an * next to it means that a recipe is included for that dish. (Any item without an * is generic food, such as French bread or a tossed salad, for which you won't need a recipe.)

♦ With each menu you'll find a menu tip that helps to cut down on preparation time or gives other useful information.

♦ Menu ingredients are always listed in the same order: pantry items first, followed by seasonings, fresh vegetables, fresh fruits, meats, dairy products, eggs, breads and frozen items.

♦ For every menu there is a timetable that gives you the order in which to prepare the meal for maximum efficiency. In many cases, dovetailing cooking times or other procedures are part of the menu plan.

♦ All of our menus are planned for four servings, with substantial portions. However, if one of your friends or family members usually eats more than one serving, you should factor this information into your meal planning.

♦ Each meal has complete nutrition information, calculated for one serving of the entire menu. Whenever a choice of ingredients is given, such as ¼ cup plain yogurt or sour cream, we provide the nutrition information for the first ingredient only. And when an ingredient such as whipped cream is listed as "if desired," it is not included in the nutrition information. You'll find a few recipes for desserts and muffins that yield more than four servings; we've calculated only one portion in the nutrition information. Serve the extra portions as snacks, or for lunch the following day.

MEAL-PLANNING POINTERS

In addition to our menus, there are many other easy ideas to help you beat the clock. Try the following:

♦ Read all the recipes for each menu and assemble all the ingredients and equipment before starting to cook.

♦ Plan for leftovers, to make a second meal quick and easy.

♦ When possible, make double portions of favorite dishes and freeze or refrigerate half for later.

♦ Try roasting two types of meat at the same time, for example, chicken and beef. Serve one hot that night and save the other to serve hot or cold the next day.

♦ Pair foods that can cook in the same pan or at the same oven temperature.

♦ When you have time prepare such staples as toasted coconut, toasted nuts, dry bread crumbs and croutons. Cover tightly and store for future use.

♦ Keep store-bought frozen chopped onion on hand, or make your own: Place peeled, chopped onion in boiling water about 1½ minutes. Chill immediately in ice water. Drain, package and freeze.

♦ If you forget to chill canned fruits or vegetables, give them a quick chill in the freezer for twenty minutes.

♦ When you want to save even more preparation time, use ingredients from your deli or a salad bar. Use cut-up vegetables for salads, crudités, a stir-fry or in specific recipes. A deli is an excellent source for prepared salads and cooked meats.

♦ Store-bought tomatoes are generally hard and need time to ripen, so always try to keep a few on hand so they'll be ripe when you want them. Tomatoes are wonderful when added to a salad, sliced and served as a side dish, and finely chopped and mixed with plain yogurt, sour cream or mayonnaise for a meat or vegetable sauce.

♦ Use your microwave to cook one item of a meal while you prepare the rest conventionally. Vegetables are excellent cooked in a microwave; it's also great to whip up a fast dessert of "baked" fruit.

♦ Get family and friends involved in meal preparation. Parcel out chopping, salad making, beverage detail, table setting even answering the phone. Meal preparation will go more quickly, and you'll enjoy the company.

SERVING IDEAS

With very little effort you can trim even more time off your dinners—and use leftovers creatively—with the tips below.

♦ Take leftovers from one meal and make them into a different dish. Try these ideas:

Cut leftover meat into small pieces and toss with salad greens and a tangy horseradish or mustard dressing for a refreshing salad.

Change the flavor of gravy and sauces by adding different herbs and spices.

Turn plain baked or boiled potatoes into a potato salad.

Toss with a vinaigrette dressing instead of mayonnaise for a new flavor. Toss with a low-calorie vinaigrette if you'd like to save calories.

When you cook pasta, double the amount. Toss half with olive oil, cover and refrigerate. You'll have the beginnings of a pasta salad for the following night.

Use leftover vegetables in omelets or salads.

Perk up sandwiches with horseradish, chilies or flavored mustards.

♦ Plain yogurt can become a side dish, sauce or dessert when it's mixed with one of the following:

Sliced cucumber for a quick, cooling cucumber salad
Hot vegetables, cracked pepper and parsley for a side dish
Shredded or finely chopped cucumber and dill weed as a sauce for fish or chicken
Tarragon for a vegetable or meat sauce
Fresh fruit, then sprinkled with brown sugar or honey for a dessert

♦ Make seasoned butters to jazz up plain vegetables. Heat ¼ cup butter or margarine over low heat until melted, then mix in one of the following ingredients:

2 tablespoons grated Parmesan cheese
¼ teaspoon curry powder
1 tablespoon prepared horseradish
1 tablespoon sesame seed and 2 tablespoons soy sauce
1 clove garlic, finely chopped

♦ Top bread slices, English muffins, corn bread or frankfurter buns with flavored butters or shredded or grated cheese and broil until bubbly.

♦ Mix ½ cup margarine or butter with 1 teaspoon dried thyme, dill weed or basil. Cover and store in the refrigerator to use for a quick bread topping.

STOCKING THE KITCHEN

A well-stocked pantry and the right cooking equipment guarantee hours saved. The right tool for the right job will keep your cooking easy and efficient. And knowing that basic ingredients are right inside your cupboard will allow you to assemble one meal after another in minutes, and eliminate unpleasant surprises when one missing ingredient throws off your whole schedule.

Below are guidelines for stocking your kitchen. We have not listed common pantry items, since you know what items you use on a regular basis. Rather, these are general guidelines to use in addition to the kitchen equipment and shopping knowledge you already have.

Equipment: No doubt you have basic kitchen equipment and know how to use it. To cut down on cooking time, you may want to use a microwave and a food processor; both are readily available in a selection of price ranges. You'll find an entire collection of microwave recipes in chapter 6.

♦ Always keep knives sharpened; cutting will be faster and safer.

♦ Use nonstick cookware and bakeware; they eliminate the need for greasing and are easier to clean.

♦ Use the correct utensils to measure ingredients. Use a glass measuring cup for liquids; graduated, nested measuring cups for dry ingredients and solid fats; graduated measuring spoons for both dry and liquid ingredients.

♦ Use the proper equipment for the task; pare vegetables with a vegetable parer, use a colander to drain pasta, kitchen shears to cut poultry or snip herbs, a basting brush for basting, a kitchen timer to keep track of cooking times and so on. If you don't have the basics, it's worth the modest investment to stock your kitchen properly.

Seasonings: Fresh herbs always add to any dish, whether homegrown or purchased. They can be quickly chopped or snipped and added to sauces, vegetables or meats. Homegrown herbs give you constant access to fresh flavor, while store-bought herbs have a rather short shelf life. If you don't grow your own, you'll want to keep dried herbs on hand, stored away from heat and sunlight.

Buying ground spices will save you time as whole spices need to be ground whenever you want to use them. Ground spices lose their flavor over time, so replace your ground spices after about eighteen months. Keep your pepper grinder filled with whole black peppercorns. A few quick twists will add zest to soups, salads, vegetables and meats.

Vegetables: Fresh vegetables are always first choice, especially when in season. However, thanks to modern technology, frozen vegetables are quite good and canned vegetables are also a great convenience. Both allow you to keep them on hand for a long time and that extends your options on days you can't stop to buy fresh produce. Many supermarkets sell cleaned and cut vegetables in their produce section, and have salad bars that offer a selection of fresh-cut vegetables. Cut vegetables will last in your refrigerator for several days.

Always keep onions and garlic in your pantry as they are infinitely useful. Onions stored in a single layer in a well-ventilated, cool place will last several months. You may want to keep frozen onions on hand, too—see page 3. Garlic stored in a well-ventilated, cool, dry place will last several weeks. You can also buy chopped garlic in

oil, which should be refrigerated after opening.

Fruits: Unless bought in season, many fruits such as peaches, plums and pears need to be purchased a few days before serving to give them time to ripen. Fruit, whole or cut, is always a satisfying dessert, so it's a good idea to keep some on hand. Use fruit as an attractive centerpiece, and help yourself to pieces as they become ripe. When very tight on time, serve berries or grapes as they don't have to be cut and seeded, or buy precut fruit at the supermarket. Watermelon, cantaloupe, honeydew and pineapple are often sold precut. Keep canned fruit on hand and chill in the freezer for twenty minutes for a quick fruit salad. Prepared applesauce can be a tasty side dish, an accompaniment to meat, or a dessert.

Dairy: Sticks of butter or margarine are more easy to measure than the tub product. However, when you want to make a flavored spread for meat, vegetables or breads, soft tub margarine is a better bet. Shredded cheeses are sold in premeasured packages; presliced and pregrated cheeses are also convenient to have on hand. Keep plain and vanilla yogurt in stock to be used for quick side dishes, sauces and desserts.

Meats and Seafood: For quick meals, you'll want to buy smaller pieces of meat, which cook faster than large pieces, such as roasts. Look for skinless, boneless turkey and chicken parts, meats that have already been cut for stir-frying or thin cuts of meat to sauté or grill. Ground meats are great to keep in the freezer. Form patties before freezing for an easy hamburger, or make meatballs. Freeze in small quantities (about one pound) to cut down on defrosting time.

Fish and shellfish cook quickly, and fillets or steaks mean no boning. Both cook beautifully in the microwave, or try them on the grill. Shellfish such as scallops and shrimp are terrific in a stir-fry; buy shrimp already cleaned and shelled. Cooked shellfish is available in many markets, and don't forget that old favorite, canned tuna. You'll also want to keep some canned salmon in the pantry.

Baked Goods. Many supermarkets have in-house bakeries that offer a very tasty and tempting array of treats. While some breads and desserts can be fixed quickly, buying baked goods takes away a time-consuming element of meal preparation. A purchased dessert can be a satisfying finish to a meal that is otherwise entirely homemade. Keep crackers on hand as the base for impromptu appetizers, and cookies in the cupboard to round out a simple dessert of fruit or ice cream or to serve alone.

CHAPTER 2

BEEF AND PORK

BROILED TENDERLOINS* • PEANUT SAUCE* • NOODLES ROMANOFF* • GREEN BEANS • ORANGE-TOSSED STRAWBERRIES*

MENU MAKES 4 SERVINGS

INGREDIENTS

¼ cup creamy peanut butter

1 tablespoon packed brown sugar

1 tablespoon lime juice

4 ounces uncooked wide noodles

1 tablespoon chopped fresh or 1 teaspoon freeze-dried chives

½ teaspoon salt

¼ teaspoon ground coriander

¼ teaspoon ground cumin

Dash of pepper

2 medium cloves garlic

3 cups strawberries

1 orange

4 beef tenderloin steaks, each 1 inch thick (about 1 pound)

1 cup sour cream

¼ cup grated Parmesan cheese

1 tablespoon margarine or butter

1 pound frozen green beans

MENU TIP: An easy, flavorful peanut sauce adds pizzazz to simple broiled meat.

TIMETABLE

1. Cook noodles for Noodles Romanoff.

2. Prepare Peanut Sauce.

3. Prepare Broiled Tenderloins.

4. Prepare green beans.

5. Prepare Orange-tossed Strawberries.

6. Finish noodles.

NUTRITION INFORMATION PER SERVING

Calories	625	**Percent of U.S. RDA**	
Protein, grams	42	Protein	64
Carbohydrate, grams	36	Vitamin A	26
Fat, grams	36	Vitamin C	100
Cholesterol, milligrams	125	Thiamin	18
Sodium, milligrams	560	Riboflavin	32
Potassium, milligrams	1000	Niacin	46
		Calcium	24
		Iron	34

BROILED TENDERLOINS

4 beef tenderloin steaks, each
   1 inch thick (about
   1 pound)
⅛ teaspoon salt
Dash of pepper

Set oven control to broil. Place beef steaks on rack in broiler pan. Place broiler pan so tops of steaks are 3 to 5 inches from heat. Broil 5 minutes or until brown. Sprinkle with salt and pepper. Turn steaks. Broil 7 to 9 minutes longer for medium doneness.

PEANUT SAUCE

½ cup water
¼ cup creamy peanut butter
1 medium clove garlic,
   chopped
1 tablespoon lime juice
¼ teaspoon ground coriander
¼ teaspoon ground cumin

Mix all ingredients in 1-quart saucepan. Heat over medium heat, stirring occasionally, until smooth and warm. Serve with Broiled Tenderloins.

NOODLES ROMANOFF

4 ounces uncooked wide
   noodles
1 cup sour cream
2 tablespoons grated
   Parmesan cheese
1 tablespoon chopped fresh
   chives
¼ teaspoon salt
Dash of pepper
1 medium clove garlic,
   crushed
1 tablespoon margarine
2 tablespoons grated
   Parmesan cheese

Cook noodles as directed on package; drain. Mix sour cream, 2 tablespoons Parmesan cheese, the chives, salt, pepper and garlic. Stir margarine into hot noodles. Stir in sour cream mixture. Place on warm platter. Sprinkle with 2 tablespoons Parmesan cheese.

ORANGE-TOSSED STRAWBERRIES

1 orange, cut in half
3 cups strawberries
1 tablespoon brown sugar

Cut strawberries in half. Squeeze juice from orange halves over strawberries. Toss strawberries and divide among 4 dessert dishes. Sprinkle with brown sugar.

MENU 2

BEEF-ORANGE STIR-FRY* ◆RICE ◆ LEMON YOGURT-FRUIT TOSS*

MENU MAKES 4 SERVINGS

INGREDIENTS

⅔ cup uncooked regular long grain or 1½ cups uncooked instant rice

3 tablespoons vegetable oil

2 tablespoons cornstarch

2 tablespoons soy sauce

1 teaspoon ground ginger

⅛ teaspoon crushed red pepper

4 medium stalks bok choy

2 medium carrots

1 small onion

2 medium cloves garlic

2 cups cut-up fresh fruit

½ teaspoon grated lemon peel

1 cup orange juice

1 pound beef boneless sirloin steak

½ cup lemon yogurt

1 package (6 ounces) frozen pea pods

MENU TIP: Buy cut-up fresh fruit from the market for Lemon Yogurt–Fruit Toss. To thaw pea pods quickly, microwave on medium 2 minutes.

TIMETABLE

1. Slice beef steak and vegetables for Beef-Orange Stir-Fry.

2. Thaw pea pods.

3. Prepare rice.

4. Prepare stir-fry.

5. Prepare Lemon Yogurt–Fruit Toss.

NUTRITION INFORMATION PER SERVING

Calories	580	**Percent of U.S. RDA**	
Protein, grams	32	Protein	48
Carbohydrate, grams	64	Vitamin A	100
Fat, grams	22	Vitamin C	100
Cholesterol, milligrams	75	Thiamin	36
Sodium, milligrams	620	Riboflavin	24
Potassium, milligrams	1060	Niacin	42
		Calcium	10
		Iron	34

BEEF-ORANGE STIR-FRY

1 pound beef boneless sirloin steak
4 medium stalks bok choy
2 medium carrots
1 tablespoon vegetable oil
1 teaspoon ground ginger
2 medium cloves garlic,
  chopped
2 tablespoons vegetable oil
1 package (6 ounces) fro-
  zen pea pods, thawed
  slightly
1 small onion, chopped
  (about ¼ cup)
1 cup orange juice
½ cup cold water
2 tablespoons cornstarch
2 tablespoons soy sauce
⅛ teaspoon crushed red
  pepper

Trim fat from beef steak. Cut beef with grain into thin 2-inch strips. Cut bok choy diagonally into ¼-inch slices; chop the green tops. Cut carrots diagonally into thin slices. Heat 12-inch skillet or wok until 1 or 2 drops of water bubble and skitter when sprinkled in skillet.

Add 1 tablespoon oil; rotate skillet to coat side. Add beef and sprinkle with ginger and garlic. Cook and stir about 3 minutes or until beef is brown. Remove beef from skillet.

Add 2 tablespoons oil to skillet; rotate skillet to coat side. Add bok choy, carrots, pea pods and onion. Cook and stir about 3 minutes or until carrots are tender. Stir in beef and orange juice; heat to boiling. Mix cold water, cornstarch, soy sauce and red pepper; stir into beef mixture. Cook and stir about 1 minute or until thickened. Serve over hot cooked rice.

LEMON YOGURT-FRUIT TOSS

½ cup lemon yogurt
½ teaspoon grated lemon
  peel
2 cups cut-up fresh fruit

Mix all ingredients in medium bowl.

STIR-FRIED FAJITAS* • LETTUCE SALAD WITH RANCH DRESSING • MEXICAN FRUIT DESSERT*

MENU MAKES 4 SERVINGS

INGREDIENTS

3 tablespoons vegetable oil

2 tablespoons powdered sugar

2 tablespoons coffee-flavored liqueur

½ cup salsa

¼ cup ranch salad dressing

1 can (11 ounces) mandarin orange segments

2 tablespoons lime juice

3 tablespoons chopped fresh cilantro

2 teaspoons chili powder

1 tablespoon chopped fresh or 1 teaspoon dried oregano

⅛ teaspoon ground cinnamon

4 cups lettuce salad

2 medium green or red bell peppers

2 large onions

2 medium cloves garlic

1 pint strawberries

1 banana

1 pound beef boneless sirloin steak

½ cup whipping (heavy) cream

8 flour tortillas (10 inches in diameter)

1 container (6 ounces) frozen guacamole

MENU TIP: Buy the lettuce salad from a salad bar. If your salad bar has strips of bell peppers, buy about 8 ounces—that will equal the 2 medium bell peppers used in the fajitas.

TIMETABLE

1. Chill bowl and beaters in freezer for whipping cream in Mexican Fruit Dessert.

2. Toss fruit with liqueur for dessert; refrigerate.

3. Prepare Stir-fried Fajitas.

4. Prepare salad.

5. Finish dessert.

NUTRITION INFORMATION PER SERVING

		Percent of U.S. RDA	
Calories	925		
Protein, grams	33	Protein	50
Carbohydrate, grams	79	Vitamin A	58
Fat, grams	54	Vitamin C	100
Cholesterol, milligrams	125	Thiamin	30
Sodium, milligrams	480	Riboflavin	34
Potassium, milligrams	1280	Niacin	40
		Calcium	26
		Iron	42

STIR-FRIED FAJITAS

8 flour tortillas (10 inches
in diameter)
1 pound beef boneless sirloin steak
1 tablespoon vegetable oil
2 tablespoons lime juice
3 tablespoons chopped fresh
cilantro
2 teaspoons chili powder
1 tablespoon chopped fresh
or 1 teaspoon dried oregano
2 medium cloves garlic,
chopped
2 tablespoons vegetable oil
2 large onions, sliced
2 medium green or red bell
peppers, cut into ¼-inch
strips
½ cup salsa
1 container (6 ounces) frozen guacamole, thawed

Heat oven to 250°. Wrap tortillas in aluminum foil or place on heatproof serving plate and cover with aluminum foil. Heat about 15 minutes or until warm. Trim fat from beef steak. Cut beef with grain into thin 2-inch strips. Heat 12-inch skillet or wok until 1 or 2 drops of water bubble and skitter when sprinkled in skillet.

Add 1 tablespoon oil; rotate skillet to coat side. Add beef and lime juice. Sprinkle with cilantro, chili powder, oregano and garlic. Cook and stir about 3 minutes or until beef is brown. Remove mixture from skillet.

Add 2 tablespoons oil to skillet; rotate skillet to coat side. Add onions and bell peppers. Cook 3 minutes or until bell peppers are crisp-tender. Stir in beef mixture. Cook 1 minute longer. For each serving, place some of the beef mixture in center of tortilla. Top with salsa and guacamole. Fold 1 end up about 1 inch over beef mixture; fold right and left sides over folded end.

MEXICAN FRUIT DESSERT

1 can (11 ounces) manda-
rin orange segments, well
drained
1 banana, sliced
1 pint strawberries, cut in
half
2 tablespoons coffee-flavored
liqueur
½ cup whipping (heavy)
cream
2 tablespoons powdered
sugar
⅛ teaspoon ground cinnamon

Toss mandarin orange segments, banana and strawberries with liqueur in medium bowl. Beat whipping cream, powdered sugar and cinnamon in chilled bowl until stiff. Divide fruit mixture among 4 dessert dishes. Serve immediately with dollops of whipped cream mixture.

◆ MENU 4 ◆

QUICK LASAGNE* ◆ HERBED ITALIAN BREAD* ◆ TOSSED SALAD WITH RIPE OLIVES AND PEPPERS

MENU MAKES 4 SERVINGS

INGREDIENTS

6 uncooked instant lasagne noodles (each about 6½ × 3 inches)

1 cup spaghetti sauce

¼ cup sliced pitted ripe olives

¼ cup pickled pepper rings

¼ cup Italian salad dressing

1 teaspoon Italian seasoning

¼ teaspoon garlic powder

3 cups salad greens

3 tablespoons chopped fresh parsley

1 medium clove garlic

½ pound ground beef

1 container (12 ounces) low-fat cottage cheese

1 cup shredded Monterey Jack cheese (4 ounces)

2 tablespoons grated Parmesan cheese

¼ cup margarine or butter

½ loaf (1-pound size) Italian or French bread

MENU TIP: This wonderful lasagne can be made in 30 minutes. It serves more easily if allowed to stand for 5 minutes. So, while the lasagne is standing, set the table and call everyone to dinner.

TIMETABLE

1. Prepare Quick Lasagne.

2. Prepare Herbed Italian Bread.

3. Toss salad.

NUTRITION INFORMATION PER SERVING

		Percent of U.S. RDA	
Calories	715		
Protein, grams	42	Protein	64
Carbohydrate, grams	49	Vitamin A	28
Fat, grams	38	Vitamin C	24
Cholesterol, milligrams	90	Thiamin	22
Sodium, milligrams	1370	Riboflavin	32
Potassium, milligrams	520	Niacin	26
		Calcium	34
		Iron	26

QUICK LASAGNE

½ pound ground beef
1 medium clove garlic,
    chopped
1 teaspoon Italian seasoning
1 cup spaghetti sauce
6 uncooked instant lasagne
    noodles, (each about
    6½ × 3 inches)
1 container (12 ounces) low-
    fat cottage cheese
1 cup shredded Monterey
    Jack cheese (4 ounces)
2 tablespoons grated
    Parmesan cheese

Heat oven to 400°. Cook ground beef and garlic in 10-inch skillet over medium heat, stirring frequently, until ground beef is brown; drain. Stir in Italian seasoning and spaghetti sauce. Heat to boiling; remove from heat.

Spread ¼ cup beef mixture in square pan, 8 × 8 × 2 or 9 × 9 × 2 inches. Top with 2 lasagne noodles. Spread one-third of the beef mixture (about ½ cup) over noodles in pan. Spread one-third of the cottage cheese (about ½ cup) over beef mixture.

Sprinkle with one-third of the Monterey Jack cheese (about ⅓ cup) on top. Repeat layering twice. Sprinkle with Parmesan cheese. Bake about 10 minutes or until hot and cheese is melted. Let stand 5 minutes before serving.

HERBED ITALIAN BREAD

½ loaf (1-pound size)
    Italian or French bread
¼ cup margarine or butter,
    softened
3 tablespoons chopped fresh
    parsley
¼ teaspoon garlic powder

Heat oven to 400°. Cut bread diagonally into 1-inch slices. Mix remaining ingredients. Spread margarine mixture over one side of cut surfaces; reassemble loaf. Wrap securely in heavy-duty aluminum foil. Bake 10 to 15 minutes or until hot.

nu #4 (page 17)

◇ Menu 5

Spicy Beef Burgers* ◆ Chili-Cheese Spread* ◆ Tortilla Chips ◆ Strawberry-Lime Slush*

MENU MAKES 4 SERVINGS

INGREDIENTS

¼ cup powdered sugar

2 tablespoons lime juice

4 ounces tortilla chips

1 can (4 ounces) chopped green chilies

½ teaspoon salt

⅛ teaspoon pepper

1 small onion

1 medium clove garlic

2 pints strawberries

1 pound ground beef

½ cup shredded Cheddar cheese (2 ounces)

2 tablespoons sour cream

4 hamburger buns

1½ cups crushed ice

MENU TIP: Use mild or hot chopped green chilies for the cheese spread, according to your preference. One can (4 ounces) chopped green chilies will be enough to prepare both the burgers and the spread. To crush ice for Strawberry-Lime Slush, place cubes in a heavy plastic freezer bag and hit with hammer.

TIMETABLE

1. Hull strawberries for Strawberry-Lime Slush.

2. Prepare Spicy Beef Burgers.

3. Prepare Chili-Cheese Spread while burgers are cooking.

4. Prepare slush.

NUTRITION INFORMATION PER SERVING

Calories	590	Percent of U.S. RDA	
Protein, grams	38	Protein	58
Carbohydrate, grams	62	Vitamin A	8
Fat, grams	21	Vitamin C	100
Cholesterol, milligrams	100	Thiamin	20
Sodium, milligrams	820	Riboflavin	32
Potassium, milligrams	800	Niacin	38
		Calcium	22
		Iron	32

SPICY BEEF BURGERS

1 pound ground beef
1 small onion, chopped
   (about ¼ cup)
2 to 3 tablespoons chopped
   green chilies
½ teaspoon salt
⅛ teaspoon pepper
1 medium clove garlic,
   chopped
4 hamburger buns

Mix all ingredients except buns. Shape beef mixture into 4 patties, each about ½ inch thick. Cook in 10-inch skillet over medium heat, turning once, about 10 minutes for medium or until desired doneness. Serve on hamburger buns with Chili-Cheese Spread.

CHILI-CHEESE SPREAD

½ cup shredded Cheddar
   cheese (2 ounces)
2 tablespoons sour cream
2 tablespoons chopped green
   chilies

Mix all ingredients. Spread about 2 tablespoons mixture over each burger.

STRAWBERRY-LIME SLUSH

2 pints strawberries
1½ cups crushed ice
¼ cup powdered sugar
2 tablespoons lime juice

Reserve 4 strawberries for garnish if desired. Wash and hull remaining strawberries. Place crushed ice and 1 pint strawberries in blender or food processor. Cover and blend on high speed 30 seconds or process until mixture is almost smooth. Pour into 1-quart (or larger) pitcher. Place remaining strawberries, the powdered sugar and lime juice in blender or food processor. Cover and blend on high speed 30 seconds or process until almost smooth.

Add mixture to pitcher; stir. Serve in 4 tall glasses. Garnish sides of glasses with reserved strawberries. Serve immediately.

SUPER PHILLY BEEF SANDWICHES* • EASY FRUIT SALAD* • TURTLE BROWNIES A LA MODE*

MENU MAKES 4 SERVINGS

INGREDIENTS

¼ cup packed brown sugar

¼ cup chopped pecans

1 tablespoon lemon juice

1 tablespoon honey

¼ teaspoon vanilla

1 can (11 ounces) mandarin orange segments

1 can (8¼ ounces) pineapple chunks in syrup

1 cup salad greens

1½ cups fresh or 1 can (4 ounces) sliced mushrooms

⅓ cup chopped green bell pepper

1 medium onion

1 cup seedless grapes

1 red apple

¾ pound thinly sliced cooked roast beef

⅔ cup plain yogurt

4 slices provolone cheese

5 tablespoons margarine or butter

4 kaiser rolls

4 brownies

1 pint vanilla ice milk

MENU TIP: Purchase the chopped bell pepper and sliced mushrooms from a salad bar. If you like your fruit salad chilled, refrigerate the canned mandarin oranges and pineapple the night before. Mix the fruit salad dressing in the bowl first, and you'll need only one bowl.

TIMETABLE

1. Prepare Caramel Sauce for Turtle Brownies a la Mode.

2. Cook vegetables for Super Philly Beef Sandwiches.

3. Prepare Easy Fruit Salad and refrigerate.

4. Assemble and broil sandwiches.

5. Assemble brownies.

NUTRITION INFORMATION PER SERVING

		Percent of U.S. RDA	
Calories	1045		
Protein, grams	46	Protein	70
Carbohydrate, grams	108	Vitamin A	28
Fat, grams	50	Vitamin C	100
Cholesterol, milligrams	140	Thiamin	38
Sodium, milligrams	850	Riboflavin	56
Potassium, milligrams	1140	Niacin	38
		Calcium	50
		Iron	36

SUPER PHILLY BEEF SANDWICHES

1 medium onion, coarsely
   chopped (about ½ cup)
1½ cups fresh or 1 can
   (4 ounces) sliced
   mushrooms
⅓ cup chopped green bell
   pepper
2 tablespoons margarine
4 kaiser rolls, split
¾ pound thinly sliced cooked
   roast beef
4 slices provolone cheese

Cook onion, mushrooms and bell pepper in margarine in 10-inch skillet over medium-high heat 5 minutes, stirring occasionally, until vegetables are tender.

Set oven control to broil. Place bottom halves of rolls on ungreased cookie sheet. Toast if desired. Top with vegetable mixture, beef and cheese.

Broil with tops 5 to 6 inches from heat 2 to 3 minutes or just until cheese is melted. Top each with remaining half roll toasted if desired.

EASY FRUIT SALAD

⅔ cup plain yogurt
1 tablespoon honey
1 tablespoon lemon juice
1 cup seedless grapes
1 can (11 ounces) mandarin orange segments
1 can (8¼ ounces) pineapple chunks in syrup
1 red apple, sliced
1 cup bite-size salad greens

Drain mandarin oranges and pineapple. Mix yogurt, honey and lemon juice in medium bowl. Stir in remaining ingredients.

TURTLE BROWNIES A LA MODE

Caramel Sauce (below)
4 brownies
1 pint vanilla ice milk
¼ cup chopped pecans

Prepare Caramel Sauce. Place brownies in dessert dishes. Top with ice milk and Caramel Sauce. Sprinkle with pecans. Serve immediately.

¼ cup packed brown sugar
2 tablespoons water
3 tablespoons margarine
¼ teaspoon vanilla

Caramel Sauce

Mix brown sugar and water in 1-quart saucepan. Heat to boiling over medium heat. Cook and stir 1 minute; remove from heat. Stir in margarine and vanilla. Cool slightly. Serve sauce warm.

TANGY STEAK SALAD* • TANGY DRESSING* • CRUSTY FRENCH BREAD

MENU MAKES 4 SERVINGS

INGREDIENTS

3 tablespoons olive or vegetable oil

2 teaspoons cornstarch

4 tablespoons Dijon mustard

3 tablespoons vinegar

1 tablespoon ketchup

1 tablespoon chopped fresh parsley

1 teaspoon chopped fresh or ½ teaspoon dried basil

¾ teaspoon salt

4 cups iceberg lettuce

1 cup sliced celery

4 green onions

1 small red bell pepper

1 pound beef boneless top sirloin steak

½ loaf (1-pound size) crusty French bread

MENU TIP: Keep a supply of torn lettuce in the refrigerator ready to use for salads. Or, buy the lettuce, celery, green onions and red bell pepper for this meal from a salad bar.

TIMETABLE

1. Prepare Tangy Dressing.

2. Heat bread, if desired.

3. Prepare Tangy Steak Salad.

NUTRITION INFORMATION PER SERVING

		Percent of U.S. RDA	
Calories	485		
Protein, grams	30	Protein	46
Carbohydrate, grams	39	Vitamin A	22
Fat, grams	23	Vitamin C	80
Cholesterol, milligrams	70	Thiamin	18
Sodium, milligrams	1050	Riboflavin	20
Potassium, milligrams	590	Niacin	32
		Calcium	8
		Iron	30

TANGY STEAK SALAD

1 tablespoon olive or vegetable oil
1 pound beef boneless top
sirloin steak, thinly
sliced
3 tablespoons Dijon mustard
1 tablespoon chopped fresh
parsley
4 cups bite-size pieces iceberg lettuce
1 cup sliced celery
4 green onions (with tops),
sliced
1 small red bell pepper,
sliced

Heat oil in 10-inch skillet over high heat until hot. Cook beef steak about 2 minutes, stirring constantly, until brown; drain. Stir in mustard and parsley; keep warm. Toss lettuce, celery, green onions and bell pepper. Divide among 4 dinner plates. Top with steak mixture.

TANGY DRESSING

¾ cup water
2 teaspoons cornstarch
3 tablespoons vinegar
2 tablespoons olive or vegetable oil
1 tablespoon ketchup
1 tablespoon Dijon mustard
1 teaspoon chopped fresh or
½ teaspoon dried basil
¾ teaspoon salt

Mix water and cornstarch in 1-quart saucepan. Heat to boiling over medium heat, stirring frequently, until mixture thickens. Cook and stir 1 minute. Stir in remaining ingredients. Heat until warm. Serve with Tangy Steak Salad.

◆ MENU 8 ◆

SAUERKRAUT-MEATBALL SOUP* ◆ DILLY CRISPS* ◆ APPLE AND PEAR COMPOTE

MENU MAKES 4 SERVINGS

INGREDIENTS

1 can (14½ ounces) Italian-style stewed tomatoes

1 can (14½ ounces) beef broth

1 can (8 ounces) sauerkraut

¼ cup ketchup

½ teaspoon caraway seed

½ teaspoon garlic powder

¼ teaspoon dried dill weed

1 apple

1 pear

2 tablespoons orange juice

1 pound ground beef

2 tablespoons margarine or butter

8 thin slices French bread

MENU TIP: This satisfying soup is especially easy, made with canned ingredients.

TIMETABLE

1. Heat oven for Dilly Crisps.

2. Shape and begin browning meatballs for Sauerkraut-Meatball Soup.

3. Prepare crisps.

4. Finish soup.

5. Slice apple and pear; drizzle with orange juice.

NUTRITION INFORMATION PER SERVING

Calories	410	**Percent of U.S. RDA**	
Protein, grams	33	Protein	50
Carbohydrate, grams	41	Vitamin A	22
Fat, grams	13	Vitamin C	50
Cholesterol, milligrams	85	Thiamin	16
Sodium, milligrams	1430	Riboflavin	20
Potassium, milligrams	840	Niacin	36
		Calcium	8
		Iron	30

SAUERKRAUT–MEATBALL SOUP

1 pound ground beef
½ teaspoon caraway seed
½ teaspoon garlic powder
1 can (14½ ounces) Italian-
   style stewed tomatoes,
   undrained
1 can (14½ ounces) beef
   broth
1 can (8 ounces) sauerkraut,
   drained
¼ cup ketchup

Mix ground beef, caraway seed and garlic powder. Shape mixture into sixteen 1½-inch meatballs. Place in 4-quart Dutch oven. Cook over medium heat until brown; drain. Stir in remaining ingredients. Heat to boiling, stirring occasionally; reduce heat. Cover and simmer 10 minutes, stirring occasionally.

DILLY CRISPS

8 thin slices French bread
2 tablespoons margarine or
   butter, softened
¼ teaspoon dried dill weed

Heat oven to 400°. Spread bread slices with margarine; sprinkle with dill weed. Place on ungreased cookie sheet. Bake about 10 minutes or until crisp.

◇ MENU 9 ◇

BURGER BEEF SOUP* • CUT-UP VEGETABLES • HARD ROLLS • APRICOT CREAM*

MENU MAKES 4 SERVINGS

INGREDIENTS

1 package (3½ ounces) vanilla instant pudding and pie filling

2 ounces uncooked egg noodles

2 cups tomato juice

1 can (17 ounces) apricot halves

1 can (10¾ ounces) condensed cream of celery soup

¾ teaspoon chopped fresh or ¼ teaspoon dried basil

¾ teaspoon chopped fresh or ¼ teaspoon dried marjoram

Ground nutmeg, if desired

⅛ teaspoon pepper

1 bay leaf

6 ounces cut-up vegetables (carrot and celery sticks, radishes, etc.)

1 small onion

1 pound ground beef

1½ cups milk

4 hard rolls

½ cup frozen peas

MENU TIP: Use frozen chopped onions for the soup. See page 3 for directions on how to make your own.

TIMETABLE

1. Prepare Burger Beef Soup.

2. Prepare Apricot Cream while soup is cooking.

NUTRITION INFORMATION PER SERVING

		Percent of U.S. RDA	
Calories	645		
Protein, grams	42	Protein	64
Carbohydrate, grams	91	Vitamin A	100
Fat, grams	13	Vitamin C	38
Cholesterol, milligrams	110	Thiamin	30
Sodium, milligrams	1810	Riboflavin	36
Potassium, milligrams	1310	Niacin	46
		Calcium	26
		Iron	38

BURGER BEEF SOUP

1 pound ground beef
1 small onion, chopped
   (about ¼ cup)
2 cups tomato juice
1¼ cups water
1 can (10¾ ounces) con-
   densed cream of celery
   soup
¾ teaspoon chopped fresh or
   ¼ teaspoon dried basil
¾ teaspoon chopped fresh or
   ¼ teaspoon dried
   marjoram
⅛ teaspoon pepper
1 bay leaf
½ cup frozen peas
2 ounces uncooked egg noodles (1 cup)

Cook ground beef and onion in 4-quart Dutch oven over medium heat about 10 minutes, stirring frequently, or until beef is brown; drain. Stir in remaining ingredients except noodles. Heat to boiling. Stir in noodles; reduce heat. Simmer uncovered about 10 minutes, stirring occasionally, until noodles are tender. Remove bay leaf.

APRICOT CREAM

1 can (17 ounces) apricot
   halves, drained
1 package (3½ ounces) va-
   nilla instant pudding
   and pie filling
1½ cups milk
Ground nutmeg, if desired

Place apricots in blender. Cover and blend until smooth. Add pudding and pie filling (dry) and milk. Cover and blend about 30 seconds, stopping blender frequently to scrape sides, until smooth and thickened. Divide among 4 dessert dishes. Sprinkle with nutmeg.

Peach Cream: Substitute 1 can (16 ounces) sliced peaches, drained, for the apricot halves.

enu #9 (page 29)

◆ Menu 10 ◆

PORK CHOPS WITH APRICOTS* ◆ ALMOND COUSCOUS* ◆ BROCCOLI

MENU MAKES 4 SERVINGS

INGREDIENTS

1 tablespoon vegetable oil

¼ cup sliced almonds

¾ cup uncooked quick-cooking couscous

1 can (16 ounces) apricot halves in light syrup

1¼ cups chicken broth

1 tablespoon steak sauce

¼ teaspoon salt

1 medium onion

1 clove garlic

4 pork loin chops, ¾ inch thick (about 1 pound)

2 tablespoons margarine or butter

1 package (16 ounces) frozen broccoli

MENU TIP: When preparing the pork chops, drain the liquid from the can of apricots directly into the skillet and you won't need a strainer. If you'd like a thicker sauce, reduce the liquid in the skillet by boiling over medium heat 3 minutes.

TIMETABLE

1. Prepare Pork Chops with Apricots.

2. Begin heating chicken broth and margarine for the Almond Couscous while sautéing the onion and garlic for the chops.

3. Prepare broccoli.

4. Finish couscous.

NUTRITION INFORMATION PER SERVING

		Percent of U.S. RDA	
Calories	600		
Protein	36	Protein	54
Carbohydrate, grams	52	Vitamin A	66
Fat, grams	28	Vitamin C	74
Cholesterol, milligrams	80	Thiamin	66
Sodium, milligrams	560	Riboflavin	36
Potassium, milligrams	1050	Niacin	44
		Calcium	10
		Iron	16

PORK CHOPS WITH APRICOTS

4 pork loin chops, ¾ inch thick (about 1 pound)
Salt
1 tablespoon vegetable oil
1 medium onion, chopped (about ½ cup)
1 clove garlic, finely chopped
1 can (16 ounces) apricot halves in light syrup, undrained
1 tablespoon steak sauce
¼ teaspoon salt

Sprinkle both sides of pork chops with salt. Heat oil in 10-inch skillet over medium heat. Cook pork chops in oil about 5 minutes on each side or until brown. Remove from skillet. Sauté onion and garlic in skillet about 3 minutes or until onion is tender. Drain syrup from apricots into skillet; stir in steak sauce and ¼ teaspoon salt. Reduce heat to medium-low. Return chops to skillet. Arrange apricot halves over pork chops. Spoon steak sauce mixture over chops and apricot halves. Cover and simmer about 3 minutes or until heated through.

ALMOND COUSCOUS

1¼ cups chicken broth
2 tablespoons margarine or butter
¾ cup uncooked quick-cooking couscous
¼ cup sliced almonds

Heat chicken broth and margarine to boiling in 1-quart saucepan. Stir in couscous and almonds. Cover; remove from heat. Let stand 5 minutes.

◇
MENU
11

PORK SCALLOPINI* ✦ PESTO VEGETABLES* ✦ FRENCH BREAD ✦ APPLESAUCE

MENU MAKES 4 SERVINGS

INGREDIENTS

½ cup finely crushed dry bread crumbs

1 teaspoon cornstarch

2 cups applesauce

1 cup dry white wine

¼ teaspoon salt

¼ teaspoon onion powder

⅛ teaspoon garlic powder

⅛ teaspoon pepper

1 pound pork tenderloin

⅓ cup pesto

¼ cup (½ stick) margarine or butter

2 tablespoons grated Parmesan cheese

1 egg

½ loaf (1-pound size) French bread

1 package (16 ounces) frozen broccoli, cauliflower and carrots

MENU TIP: Round out this meal with bakery bread and prepared applesauce to eliminate preparing extra dishes. If available, buy the pork already sliced for scallopini.

TIMETABLE

1. Prepare Pork Scallopini.

2. Prepare Pesto Vegetables while pork is cooking.

3. Heat bread, if desired.

NUTRITION INFORMATION PER SERVING

		Percent of U.S. RDA	
Calories	770		
Protein, grams	39	Protein	60
Carbohydrate, grams	77	Vitamin A	100
Fat, grams	33	Vitamin C	40
Cholesterol, milligrams	140	Thiamin	72
Sodium, milligrams	930	Riboflavin	42
Potassium, milligrams	1030	Niacin	36
		Calcium	26
		Iron	34

PORK SCALLOPINI

1 pound pork tenderloin
1 egg, slightly beaten
1 tablespoon water
½ cup finely crushed dry
    bread crumbs
¼ teaspoon salt
¼ teaspoon onion powder
⅛ teaspoon garlic powder
⅛ teaspoon pepper
2 tablespoons margarine or
    butter
1 cup dry white wine
2 tablespoons margarine or
    butter
1 teaspoon cornstarch
1 tablespoon water

Remove excess fat from pork. Cut pork diagonally into ½-inch slices. Mix egg and 1 tablespoon water. Mix bread crumbs, salt, onion powder, garlic powder and pepper. Toss pork with egg mixture. Coat with crumb mixture.

Heat 2 tablespoons margarine in 12-inch skillet over medium heat until hot. Cook pork in margarine about 8 minutes or until done. Remove pork from skillet; keep warm.

Stir wine and 2 tablespoons margarine into skillet. Heat to boiling. Mix cornstarch and 1 tablespoon water; stir into wine mixture. Cook and stir 1 minute. Pour sauce over pork.

PESTO VEGETABLES

1 package (16 ounces) frozen broccoli, cauliflower and carrots
⅓ cup pesto
2 tablespoons grated
    Parmesan cheese

Cook vegetables as directed on package; drain. Toss with pesto. Sprinkle with Parmesan cheese.

◆ MENU
12 ◆

SICHUAN STIR-FRIED PORK WITH VEGETABLES* ◆ RICE ◆ PINEAPPLE COMPOTE* ◆ GINGER TEA*

MENU MAKES 4 SERVINGS

INGREDIENTS

¼ cup golden raisins or dried cranberries

¼ cup packed brown sugar

1 tablespoon granulated sugar

1 tablespoon cornstarch

2 tablespoons vegetable oil

⅔ cup uncooked regular long grain or 1½ cups uncooked instant rice

1 tablespoon orange-flavored liqueur

1 tea bag

¼ cup chicken broth or water

2 teaspoons chili paste or chili puree with garlic

1 teaspoon soy sauce

½ teaspoon salt

⅛ teaspoon white pepper

3 cups cut-up vegetables for stir-fry

1 clove garlic

2 cups fresh pineapple chunks or 1 can (20 ounces) pineapple chunks in juice

1-inch piece unpared gingerroot

1 pound pork for stir-fry or chow mein

2 tablespoons margarine or butter

MENU TIP: Purchasing pork already cut for stir-fry or coarsely ground for chow mein is a quick way to make this stir-fry dish without the work of cutting up meat. Check your produce section for already cut-up vegetables to use in the stir-fry.

TIMETABLE

1. Slice gingerroot for Ginger Tea.

2. Mix cornstarch with water and toss pork with ingredients listed for Sichuan Stir-fried Pork with Vegetables.

3. Prepare rice.

4. Prepare Pineapple Compote.

5. Prepare tea.

6. Stir-fry pork and vegetables.

NUTRITION INFORMATION PER SERVING

		Percent of U.S. RDA	
Calories	680		
Protein, grams	31	Protein	48
Carbohydrate, grams	76	Vitamin A	100
Fat, grams	27	Vitamin C	32
Cholesterol, milligrams	90	Thiamin	60
Sodium, milligrams	600	Riboflavin	28
Potassium, milligrams	930	Niacin	36
		Calcium	8
		Iron	28

Menu #12 (page 37)

Ch'a Ching
Tea

SICHUAN STIR-FRIED PORK WITH VEGETABLES

2 teaspoons cornstarch
2 teaspoons cold water
1 pound pork for stir-fry or
  chow mein
1 teaspoon cornstarch
1 teaspoon soy sauce
½ teaspoon salt
⅛ teaspoon white pepper
2 tablespoons vegetable oil
1 clove garlic, finely chopped
3 cups cut-up vegetables for
  stir-fry
2 teaspoons chili paste or
  chili puree with garlic*
¼ cup chicken broth or water

Mix 2 teaspoons cornstarch and the water; reserve. Toss pork, 1 teaspoon cornstarch, the soy sauce, salt and white pepper.

Heat wok or 12-inch skillet until 1 or 2 drops of water bubble and skitter when sprinkled in wok.

Add oil; rotate wok to coat sides. Add pork and garlic; stir-fry until pork is no longer pink. Add vegetables; stir-fry 2 minutes. Stir in chili paste. Stir in chicken broth; heat to boiling. Stir in reserved cornstarch mixture. Cook and stir about 10 seconds or until thickened.

*1 teaspoon finely chopped dried chili pepper and 1 tablespoon soy sauce can be substituted for the chili paste.

PINEAPPLE COMPOTE

2 tablespoons margarine or
  butter
2 cups fresh pineapple
  chunks*
¼ cup packed brown sugar
¼ cup golden raisins or dried
  cranberries
1 tablespoon orange-flavored
  liqueur

Heat margarine in 1½-quart saucepan over medium heat. Stir in pineapple, brown sugar and raisins. Cook about 3 minutes, stirring constantly, until sugar is dissolved and pineapple is heated through. Stir in liqueur.

*1 can (20 ounces) pineapple chunks in juice, drained, can be substituted for the fresh pineapple.

GINGER TEA

1 tea bag
1-inch piece unpared
  gingerroot, thinly sliced
1 tablespoon granulated
  sugar
1 quart boiling water

Place tea bag, gingerroot and sugar in teapot. Cover with boiling water. Let stand 5 minutes.

HONEY-MUSTARD HAM* • RICE WITH PINE NUTS AND RAISINS* • SUGAR SNAP PEAS

MENU MAKES 4 SERVINGS

INGREDIENTS

¼ cup raisins

2 tablespoons pine nuts (1 ounce)

2 tablespoons honey

1½ cups uncooked instant rice

1½ cups chicken broth

1 tablespoon Dijon mustard

⅛ teaspoon pepper

1 green onion (with top)

1 pound fully cooked smoked ham slice (about 1 inch thick)

½ cup sour cream

1½ teaspoons margarine or butter

1 package (8 ounces) frozen sugar snap peas or 8 ounces fresh sugar snap peas

MENU TIP: Cutting the ham into serving pieces before cooking reduces the cooking time.

TIMETABLE

1. Prepare Honey-Mustard Ham.

2. Prepare Rice with Pine Nuts and Raisins.

3. Prepare sugar snap peas.

NUTRITION INFORMATION PER SERVING

		Percent of U.S. RDA	
Calories	515		
Protein, grams	30	Protein	46
Carbohydrate, grams	56	Vitamin A	16
Fat, grams	19	Vitamin C	40
Cholesterol, milligrams	75	Thiamin	96
Sodium, milligrams	1830	Riboflavin	26
Potassium, milligrams	770	Niacin	52
		Calcium	6
		Iron	24

HONEY-MUSTARD HAM

¼ cup water
2 tablespoons honey
1 tablespoon Dijon mustard
1 pound fully cooked smoked
   ham slice (about 1 inch
   thick), cut into 4 serving pieces
½ cup sour cream
1 green onion (with top),
   sliced

Mix water, honey and mustard in 10-inch skillet. Add ham. Cover and heat to boiling; reduce heat. Simmer over low heat about 15 minutes, turning once, until ham is heated through. Remove ham; keep warm. Stir in sour cream and heat 1 minute. Pour over ham. Sprinkle with green onion.

RICE WITH PINE NUTS AND RAISINS

1½ cups uncooked instant
   rice
1½ teaspoons margarine or
   butter
1½ cups chicken broth
¼ cup raisins
2 tablespoons pine nuts
   (1 ounce)
⅛ teaspoon pepper

Cook rice with margarine as directed on package except substitute chicken broth for the water and omit salt. Stir in raisins, pine nuts and pepper.

PORK PATTIES* • YOGURT SWEET POTATOES* • CRAN-APPLE SAUCE*

MENU MAKES 4 SERVINGS

INGREDIENTS

¼ cup dry bread crumbs

2 tablespoons pecan pieces

1 tablespoon molasses

¾ cup whole berry cran-berry sauce

1 can (18 ounces) vacuum-packed sweet potatoes

½ teaspoon garlic salt

½ teaspoon fennel seed

¼ teaspoon ground sage

⅛ teaspoon salt

⅛ teaspoon pepper

½ teaspoon grated lemon peel

1 small eating apple

1 pound ground pork

½ cup vanilla yogurt

1 tablespoon margarine or butter

1 egg

MENU TIP: When you make the Pork Patties, beat the egg in a large bowl, then the other ingredients. This way you'll only use one bowl.

TIMETABLE

1. Prepare Cran-Apple Sauce

2. Prepare Pork Patties.

3. Prepare Yogurt Sweet Potatoes.

NUTRITION INFORMATION PER SERVING

Calories	545	**Percent of U.S. RDA**	
Protein, grams	29	Protein	44
Carbohydrate, grams	62	Vitamin A	100
Fat, grams	20	Vitamin C	12
Cholesterol, milligrams	140	Thiamin	44
Sodium, milligrams	590	Riboflavin	30
Potassium, milligrams	760	Niacin	28
		Calcium	10
		Iron	16

PORK PATTIES

1 egg
1 pound ground pork
¼ cup dry bread crumbs
½ teaspoon garlic salt
½ teaspoon fennel seed
¼ teaspoon ground sage
⅛ teaspoon pepper

Beat egg slightly in large bowl. Stir in remaining ingredients until well blended. Shape mixture into 4 patties, each about ½ inch thick. Cook patties in 10-inch skillet over medium heat about 10 minutes, turning once, until done.

YOGURT SWEET POTATOES

1 can (18 ounces) vacuum-
packed sweet potatoes
½ cup vanilla yogurt
1 tablespoon molasses
1 tablespoon margarine or
butter
⅛ teaspoon salt
2 tablespoons pecan pieces

Mash sweet potatoes in 2-quart saucepan until no lumps remain. Stir in remaining ingredients except pecans. Heat over medium heat 6 to 7 minutes, stirring frequently, until heated through. Sprinkle with pecans.

CRAN-APPLE SAUCE

¾ cup whole berry cran-
berry sauce
1 small eating apple, finely
chopped
½ teaspoon grated lemon
peel

Mix all ingredients.

HAM-PINEAPPLE SANDWICHES* ◆
HARVEST YOGURT*

MENU MAKES 4 SERVINGS

INGREDIENTS

2 tablespoons chopped pecans

1 tablespoon honey

1 cup applesauce

1 can (8¼ ounces) crushed pineapple

¼ cup mayonnaise or salad dressing

¼ teaspoon pumpkin pie spice or ground cinnamon

4 lettuce leaves

4 slices fully cooked smoked ham or 1 can (6¾ ounces) chunk ham

1 cup vanilla yogurt

8 slices whole wheat bread

MENU TIP: Prepared fruits such as canned pineapple and applesauce bring the sweet, fresh flavor of fruit to meals without the work of peeling and chopping. Broil the 8 slices of bread for the sandwiches at one time to make the toast more quickly.

TIMETABLE

1. Prepare Harvest Yogurt; refrigerate until serving time.

2. Prepare Ham-Pineapple Sandwiches.

NUTRITION INFORMATION PER SERVING

Calories	435	**Percent of U.S. RDA**	
Protein, grams	15	Protein	22
Carbohydrate, grams	52	Vitamin A	2
Fat, grams	20	Vitamin C	12
Cholesterol, milligrams	30	Thiamin	38
Sodium, milligrams	890	Riboflavin	16
Potassium, milligrams	470	Niacin	18
		Calcium	12
		Iron	10

HAM-PINEAPPLE SANDWICHES

8 slices whole wheat bread,
    toasted
¼ cup mayonnaise or salad
    dressing
1 can (8¼ ounces) crushed
    pineapple, drained
4 slices fully cooked smoked
    ham or 1 can (6¾ ounces)
    chunk ham
4 lettuce leaves

Spread toast with mayonnaise. Spread pineapple over mayonnaise; top with ham and lettuce. Top with remaining slices toast.

HARVEST YOGURT

1 cup vanilla yogurt
1 cup applesauce
1 tablespoon honey
¼ teaspoon pumpkin pie
    spice or ground cinnamon
2 tablespoons chopped pecans

Mix yogurt, applesauce, honey and pumpkin pie spice. Spoon into 4 small dessert dishes. Sprinkle with pecans.

PICANTE PORK CHILI* • BROILED LETTUCE SALADS* • CORN MUFFINS

MENU MAKES 4 SERVINGS

INGREDIENTS

1 cup salsa

¼ cup buttermilk salad dressing

1 can (16 ounces) whole tomatoes

1 can (16 ounces) pinto beans

1 teaspoon chili powder

¼ teaspoon salt

2 slices firm iceburg lettuce, each 1 inch thick

1 large tomato

1 medium green bell pepper

1 medium onion

1 green onion

1 clove garlic

½ pound ground pork

¼ cup shredded Cheddar or process American cheese (1 ounce)

4 corn muffins

MENU TIP: Using canned pinto beans and bottled salsa is a quick way to get the flavor of long-simmered chili without a long cooking time.

TIMETABLE

1. Chop onion, garlic and bell pepper for Picante Pork Chili.

2. Cook onion, garlic, bell pepper and pork for chili.

3. Slice lettuce, tomato and green onion for Broiled Lettuce Salads.

4. Add remaining ingredients to chili.

5. Assemble and broil salads.

NUTRITION INFORMATION PER SERVING

Calories	530	**Percent of U.S. RDA**	
Protein, grams	25	Protein	38
Carbohydrate, grams	53	Vitamin A	62
Fat, grams	26	Vitamin C	74
Cholesterol, milligrams	100	Thiamin	50
Sodium, milligrams	1580	Riboflavin	30
Potassium, milligrams	1070	Niacin	32
		Calcium	22
		Iron	44

PICANTE PORK CHILI

1 medium onion, chopped
  (about ½ cup)
1 medium green bell pep-
  per, chopped (about
  1 cup)
1 clove garlic, finely chopped
½ pound ground pork
1 cup salsa
1 teaspoon chili powder
¼ teaspoon salt
1 can (16 ounces) pinto
  beans, rinsed and drained
1 can (16 ounces) whole tomatoes, undrained

Cook onion, bell pepper, garlic and pork in 3-quart sauce-pan over medium heat, stirring frequently, until pork is no longer pink; drain if necessary. Stir in remaining ingredients, breaking up tomatoes. Cover and simmer 10 minutes.

BROILED LETTUCE SALADS

2 slices firm iceburg lettuce,
  each 1 inch thick
1 large tomato, cut into
  8 wedges
¼ cup buttermilk salad
  dressing
¼ cup shredded Cheddar or
  process American cheese
  (1 ounce)
1 green onion (with top),
  sliced

Set oven control to broil. Cut lettuce slices in half; place on rack in broiler pan. Place 2 tomato wedges on each piece of lettuce. Spoon 1 tablespoon dressing over tomatoes on each salad. Sprinkle cheese over lettuce and tomatoes. Broil with tops of tomatoes about 3 inches from heat 2 to 3 minutes or until dressing and cheese bubble. Sprinkle with green onion.

CHUTNEY-HAM PITAS* • STUFFED APPLE HALVES* • FROZEN YOGURT FLOATS*

MENU MAKES 4 SERVINGS

INGREDIENTS

2 tablespoons finely chopped walnuts

2 tablespoons finely chopped raisins

1 tablespoon packed brown sugar

½ teaspoon granulated sugar

½ cup mango chutney

1 cup apple juice or cider

24 ounces club soda

¼ teaspoon dry mustard

3 whole cloves

Ground nutmeg or cardamom, if desired

1 cup finely shredded cabbage

2 medium red-skinned cooking apples

1 cup diced fully cooked smoked ham (about 6 ounces)

¼ cup plain yogurt or sour cream

1 tablespoon margarine or butter

2 pita breads (6 inches in diameter)

1 pint vanilla frozen yogurt

MENU TIP: Cutting the apples in half decreases their cooking time, as does cooking them on the stove top. Wet your knife with water to chop the raisins easily. Purchase shredded cabbage and diced ham for the Chutney-Ham Pitas from the salad bar or produce section of your market to save on chopping time.

TIMETABLE

1. Cut and core apples, chop raisins and nuts for Stuffed Apple Halves.

2. Prepare Stuffed Apple Halves.

3. Shred cabbage and dice ham for Chutney-Ham Pitas.

4. Prepare Chutney-Ham Pitas.

5. Prepare Frozen Yogurt Floats.

NUTRITION INFORMATION PER SERVING

Calories	540	**Percent of U.S. RDA**	
Protein, grams	18	Protein	28
Carbohydrate, grams	92	Vitamin A	4
Fat, grams	10	Vitamin C	20
Cholesterol, milligrams	25	Thiamin	30
Sodium, milligrams	830	Riboflavin	32
Potassium, milligrams	540	Niacin	10
		Calcium	40
		Iron	8

Chutney-Ham Pitas

1 cup finely shredded cabbage
¼ cup plain yogurt or sour cream
½ teaspoon granulated sugar
¼ teaspoon dry mustard
½ cup mango chutney
1 cup diced fully cooked smoked ham (about 6 ounces)
2 pita breads (6 inches in diameter)

Mix cabbage, yogurt, sugar and mustard. Heat mango chutney and ham over medium heat, stirring occasionally, until hot. Cut pita breads in half to form pockets. Fill each half with ham mixture. Spread cabbage mixture over ham mixture.

Stuffed Apple Halves

2 medium red-skinned cooking apples, cut in half
2 tablespoons finely chopped raisins
2 tablespoons finely chopped walnuts
1 tablespoon packed brown sugar
1 tablespoon margarine or butter
1 cup apple juice or cider
3 whole cloves

Remove cores from apple halves with melon baller or spoon. Mix raisins, walnuts, brown sugar and margarine. Press mixture in apple halves. Place apple juice, cloves and apple halves with cut sides up in 10-inch skillet. Heat apple juice to boiling; reduce heat. Cover and simmer 12 to 14 minutes or until apples are tender.

Frozen Yogurt Floats

1 pint vanilla frozen yogurt
24 ounces club soda
Ground nutmeg or
    cardamom, if desired

Scoop yogurt into 4 tall glasses. Fill with club soda. Sprinkle with nutmeg.

Menu #27 (page 79)

CHAPTER 3
CHICKEN AND TURKEY

Lemon Chicken* • Couscous with Fruit* • Italian Beans • Strawberry Ladyfingers*

MENU MAKES 4 SERVINGS

INGREDIENTS

1 cup uncooked quick-cooking couscous

½ cup diced dried fruits and raisins

4 tablespoons orange- or raspberry-flavored liqueur

1½ cups chicken broth

½ cup dry white wine or chicken broth

1 tablespoon lemon juice

½ teaspoon salt

2 tablespoons sliced green onions

1 cup strawberries

1 lemon

4 small skinless boneless chicken breast halves (about 1 pound)

½ cup strawberry yogurt

3 tablespoons margarine or butter

8 ladyfingers

1 package (10 ounces) frozen Italian beans

MENU TIP: Canned chicken broth, diced dried fruits and raisins combine with quick-cooking couscous for a tasty side dish.

TIMETABLE

1. Begin browning chicken for Lemon Chicken.

2. Prepare Italian beans.

3. Prepare Couscous with Fruit.

4. Prepare Strawberry Ladyfingers.

5. Finish chicken.

NUTRITION INFORMATION PER SERVING

		Percent of U.S. RDA	
Calories	665		
Protein, grams	37	Protein	56
Carbohydrate, grams	81	Vitamin A	16
Fat, grams	15	Vitamin C	20
Cholesterol, milligrams	145	Thiamin	12
Sodium, milligrams	819	Riboflavin	16
Potassium, milligrams	620	Niacin	76
		Calcium	8
		Iron	12

LEMON CHICKEN

2 tablespoons margarine or
    butter
4 small skinless boneless
    chicken breast halves
    (about 1 pound)
½ cup dry white wine or
    chicken broth
1 tablespoon lemon juice
¼ teaspoon salt
1 lemon, thinly sliced
2 tablespoons sliced green
    onions (with tops)

Heat margarine in 10-inch skillet until melted. Cook chicken in margarine over medium heat about 10 minutes or until brown on both sides. Add wine and lemon juice. Sprinkle with salt. Place lemon slices on chicken. Heat to boiling; reduce heat.

Cover and simmer 10 to 15 minutes or until chicken is done. Remove chicken; keep warm. Heat wine mixture to boiling. Cook 3 minutes or until reduced to about half. Pour over chicken. Sprinkle with green onions.

COUSCOUS WITH FRUIT

1½ cups chicken broth
½ cup diced dried fruit and
    raisins
1 tablespoon margarine or butter
¼ teaspoon salt
1 cup uncooked quick-
    cooking couscous

Heat chicken broth, fruit bits, margarine and salt to boiling. Stir in couscous. Cover; remove from heat. Let stand 5 minutes or until liquid is absorbed. Stir before serving.

STRAWBERRY LADYFINGERS

8 ladyfingers
4 tablespoons orange- or
    raspberry-flavored liqueur
½ cup strawberry yogurt
1 cup strawberries, cut in
    half

Divide ladyfingers among 4 dessert plates. Sprinkle each plate of ladyfingers with 1 tablespoon liqueur. Just before serving, fill or top with yogurt and strawberries.

CURRIED CHICKEN THIGHS* • BROWN RICE • PEAS • ORANGE-glazed BANANAS*

MENU MAKES 4 SERVINGS

INGREDIENTS

¼ cup raisins

2 tablespoons flaked coconut

1 tablespoon vegetable oil

1½ cups uncooked instant brown rice

1 teaspoon curry powder

½ teaspoon salt

Dash of ground ginger

Dash of ground cumin

1 small onion

2 bananas

4 skinless boneless chicken thighs (about 1 pound)

½ cup sour cream

⅓ cup orange juice

1 package (10 ounces) frozen peas

MENU TIP: Brown rice doesn't have to be time-consuming. Instant brown rice will give you the same nutty chewiness in almost no time.

TIMETABLE

1. Heat oven for Orange-glazed Bananas.

2. Start browning chicken for Curried Chicken Thighs.

3. Prepare bananas.

4. Prepare brown rice; prepare peas.

5. Finish chicken.

6. Prepare Orange-glazed Bananas; place in oven 10 minutes before end of meal.

NUTRITION INFORMATION PER SERVING

			Percent of U.S. RDA	
Calories	825			
Protein, grams	52	Protein		80
Carbohydrate, grams	114	Vitamin A		18
Fat, grams	18	Vitamin C		24
Cholesterol, milligrams	170	Thiamin		56
Sodium, milligrams	520	Riboflavin		32
Potassium, milligrams	990	Niacin		84
		Calcium		8
		Iron		38

CURRIED CHICKEN THIGHS

*4 skinless boneless chicken
   thighs (about 1 pound)*
1 tablespoon vegetable oil
1 teaspoon curry powder
½ teaspoon salt
Dash of ground ginger
Dash of ground cumin
*1 small onion, chopped
   (about ¼ cup)*
⅓ cup water
½ cup sour cream

Cut chicken thighs into 1-inch strips. Heat oil in 10-inch skillet until hot. Cook chicken in oil over medium-high heat until brown on all sides. Sprinkle with remaining ingredients except sour cream; reduce heat. Cover and simmer about 10 minutes or until chicken is done. Stir in sour cream.

ORANGE–GLAZED BANANAS

2 bananas, sliced
¼ cup raisins
⅓ cup orange juice
2 tablespoons flaked coconut

Heat oven to 375°. Mix bananas, raisins and orange juice in 1-quart casserole. Sprinkle with coconut. Bake 10 minutes or until coconut is golden brown.

Menu #20 (page 62)

QUICK BARBECUED CHICKEN WINGS* ◆ POTATO-CORN SALAD* ◆ BREAD AND BUTTER PICKLES ◆ LEMONADE TEA*

MENU MAKES 4 SERVINGS

INGREDIENTS

1 tablespoon honey

2 cups iced tea

1 can (11 ounces) corn with red and green peppers

4 ounces bread and butter pickles

½ cup chili sauce

1 tablespoon soy sauce

½ teaspoon dry mustard

¼ teaspoon ground red pepper (cayenne)

⅛ teaspoon ground cumin

Fresh mint, if desired

2 pounds chicken drummettes

1 can (6 ounces) frozen lemonade

1 pint deli potato salad

MENU TIP: Place lemonade in refrigerator the night before to thaw, or microwave opened can (if it contains no metal) on medium for about 2 minutes. Three teaspoons instant tea and 2 cups cold water can be used to make the tea if you don't have brewed iced tea on hand.

TIMETABLE

1. Prepare Quick Barbecued Chicken Wings.

2. Prepare Potato-Corn Salad.

3. Prepare Lemonade Tea.

NUTRITION INFORMATION PER SERVING

		Percent of U.S. RDA	
Calories	700		
Protein, grams	49	Protein	74
Carbohydrate, grams	58	Vitamin A	20
Fat, grams	29	Vitamin C	30
Cholesterol, milligrams	250	Thiamin	18
Sodium, milligrams	1750	Riboflavin	36
Potassium, milligrams	1030	Niacin	72
		Calcium	6
		Iron	26

Quick Barbecued Chicken Wings

2 pounds chicken drummettes
½ cup chili sauce
1 tablespoon honey
1 tablespoon soy sauce
½ teaspoon dry mustard
¼ teaspoon ground red pepper (cayenne)

Place drummettes in 10-inch nonstick skillet. Mix remaining ingredients; spoon over drummettes. Heat to boiling; reduce heat. Cover and cook over medium-low heat 20 to 25 minutes, stirring occasionally, until chicken is done.

Potato-Corn Salad

1 pint deli potato salad
1 can (11 ounces) corn with red and green peppers, drained
⅛ teaspoon ground cumin

Gently mix all ingredients.

Lemonade Tea

1 can (6 ounces) frozen lemonade, thawed
2 cups iced tea
Fresh mint, if desired

Prepare lemonade as directed on can. Stir in tea. Serve over ice. Garnish with mint.

CHICKEN-CHUTNEY STIR-FRY* ◆ RICE ◆ PEARS WITH QUICK CRÈME FRAÎCHE*

MENU MAKES 4 SERVINGS

INGREDIENTS

1 tablespoon cornstarch

1 tablespoon vegetable oil

1½ cups uncooked instant rice

¼ cup chopped peanuts

½ cup chutney

1 tablespoon soy sauce

Dash of freshly grated or ground nutmeg

2 carrots

½ medium red bell pepper

6 ounces pea pods

2 ripe pears

3 skinless boneless chicken breast halves (about 1 pound)

½ cup sour cream

2 tablespoons milk

MENU TIP: Use 1 package (6 ounces) frozen pea pods, thawed, for the Chicken-Chutney Stir-Fry. To thaw, place pea pods in cold water. Buy the crème fraîche if your grocery store carries it.

TIMETABLE

1. Heat water for rice.

2. Prepare Chicken-Chutney Stir-Fry.

3. Prepare rice.

4. Prepare Pears with Quick Crème Fraîche.

NUTRITION INFORMATION PER SERVING

Calories	670	**Percent of U.S. RDA**	
Protein, grams	38	Protein	58
Carbohydrate, grams	86	Vitamin A	100
Fat, grams	17	Vitamin C	34
Cholesterol, milligrams	80	Thiamin	38
Sodium, milligrams	420	Riboflavin	16
Potassium, milligrams	910	Niacin	86
		Calcium	10
		Iron	24

CHICKEN-CHUTNEY STIR-FRY

1 tablespoon vegetable oil
3 skinless boneless chicken
 breast halves (about 1
 pound), cut into 1-inch
 pieces
2 carrots, thinly sliced (about
 1 cup)
½ medium red bell pepper,
 cut into thin strips
1 tablespoon cornstarch
1 tablespoon soy sauce
½ cup chutney
6 ounces pea pods
¼ cup chopped peanuts

Heat oil in 10-inch skillet or wok until hot. Add chicken, carrots and bell pepper. Stir-fry over medium-high heat 5 to 7 minutes or until chicken is white. Mix cornstarch, soy sauce and chutney. Stir into chicken mixture. Cook and stir over medium heat until slightly thickened. Stir in pea pods; heat until hot. Serve over rice. Sprinkle with peanuts.

PEARS WITH QUICK CRÈME FRAÎCHE

2 ripe pears, halved with
 cores removed
Quick Crème Fraîche
 (below)
Dash of freshly grated or
 ground nutmeg

½ cup sour cream
2 tablespoons milk

Slice each pear half into thin slices and arrange on 4 dessert plates. Prepare Quick Crème Fraîche. Spoon about 2 tablespoons over pear slices on each plate. Sprinkle with nutmeg.

Quick Crème Fraîche

Mix ingredients in small bowl.

MENU 22

LINGUINE WITH CHICKEN AND ARTICHOKES* •
ORANGE WEDGES • HARD ROLLS WITH
SAVORY BUTTER*

MENU MAKES 4 SERVINGS

INGREDIENTS

2 tablespoons olive or vegetable oil

6 ounces uncooked linguine or spaghetti

1 jar (6 ounces) marinated artichoke hearts

1 tablespoon chopped fresh or 1 teaspoon dried oregano

1/4 teaspoon dried basil

Dash of rubbed sage

Dash of onion salt

1/4 teaspoon pepper

1 medium onion

1 orange

2 cups cut-up cooked chicken

2 ounces fully cooked smoked ham

1 container (8 ounces) sour cream

2 tablespoons margarine or butter

4 hard rolls

1 cup frozen peas

MENU TIP: Purchase frozen cut-up, cooked chicken or cooked chicken from the deli. The linguine is also a great way to use leftover cooked chicken.

TIMETABLE

1. Heat water and cook linguine for Linguine with Chicken and Artichokes.

2. Cut orange into 8 wedges.

3. Prepare Savory Butter.

4. Heat hard rolls, if desired.

5. Finish chicken.

NUTRITION INFORMATION PER SERVING

		Percent of U.S. RDA	
Calories	765		
Protein, grams	35	Protein	54
Carbohydrate, grams	74	Vitamin A	18
Fat, grams	36	Vitamin C	22
Cholesterol, milligrams	90	Thiamin	58
Sodium, milligrams	730	Riboflavin	36
Potassium, milligrams	580	Niacin	52
		Calcium	18
		Iron	26

LINGUINE WITH CHICKEN AND ARTICHOKES

6 ounces uncooked linguine
   or spaghetti
1 jar (6 ounces) marinated
   artichoke hearts
2 tablespoons olive or vegetable oil
1 medium onion, coarsely
   chopped (about ½ cup)
2 cups cut-up cooked chicken
1 cup frozen green peas
2 ounces sliced fully cooked
   smoked ham, cut into
   ¼-inch strips (½ cup)
1 tablespoon chopped fresh
   or 1 teaspoon dried
   oregano
¼ teaspoon pepper
1 container (8 ounces) sour
   cream

Cook linguine as directed on package; drain.

Drain liquid from artichoke hearts into 10-inch skillet; cut artichoke hearts in half and reserve. Add oil to artichoke liquid. Cook and stir onion in oil mixture until tender.

Stir artichoke hearts, chicken, peas, ham, oregano and pepper into onion mixture. Cook and stir until hot; remove from heat. Stir in sour cream. Toss hot linguine with sauce.

SAVORY BUTTER

2 tablespoons margarine or
   butter, softened
¼ teaspoon dried basil
Dash of rubbed sage
Dash of onion salt

Mix margarine, basil, sage and onion salt. Serve with hard rolls.

MENU
23

OPEN-FACE PITA SANDWICHES* • CUT-UP VEGETABLES • CLUSTERS OF GREEN GRAPES • RASPBERRY FROST SODAS*

MENU MAKES 4 SERVINGS

INGREDIENTS

½ jar (8-ounce size) sun-dried tomatoes in oil

1 cup cranberry juice

1 can (12 ounces) ginger ale

¼ teaspoon Italian seasoning

1 small onion

Cut-up vegetables

¼ pound green grapes

4 small skinless boneless chicken breast halves (about 1 pound)

½ cup shredded mozzarella cheese (2 ounces)

¼ cup grated Parmesan cheese

2 whole wheat pita breads (6 inches in diameter)

1 pint raspberry sherbet

MENU TIP: Buy skinless, boneless chicken breasts, and vegetables already cut up if you don't have a supply ready in the refrigerator. Put the cranberry juice and ginger ale in the refrigerator the night before.

TIMETABLE

1. Prepare Open-Face Pita Sandwiches.

2. Prepare grapes while sandwiches are baking.

3. Place vegetables on serving plate.

4. Just before serving, prepare Raspberry Frost Sodas.

NUTRITION INFORMATION PER SERVING

		Percent of U.S. RDA	
Calories	580		
Protein, grams	36	Protein	54
Carbohydrate, grams	72	Vitamin A	100
Fat, grams	16	Vitamin C	44
Cholesterol, milligrams	80	Thiamin	12
Sodium, milligrams	250	Riboflavin	16
Potassium, milligrams	720	Niacin	64
		Calcium	18
		Iron	10

OPEN-FACE PITA SANDWICHES

½ jar (8-ounce size) sun-
  dried tomatoes in oil,
  drained and 2 tablespoons
  oil reserved
4 small skinless boneless
  chicken breast halves
  (about 1 pound), cut into
  about ½-inch pieces
¼ teaspoon Italian seasoning
1 small onion, thinly sliced
¼ cup grated Parmesan
  cheese
2 whole wheat pita breads
  (6 inches in diameter)
½ cup shredded mozzarella
  cheese (2 ounces)

Heat oven to 375°. Heat reserved oil in 10-inch skillet over medium-high heat until hot. Sauté chicken, Italian seasoning and onion in oil about 4 minutes, stirring frequently, until chicken turns white. Cut tomatoes into ¼-inch strips. Stir tomatoes and Parmesan cheese into chicken mixture.

Split each pita bread in half around edge with knife to make 4 rounds. Divide chicken mixture evenly among rounds. Sprinkle with mozzarella cheese. Bake about 5 minutes or until cheese is melted.

RASPBERRY FROST SODAS

1 cup cranberry juice, chilled
1 pint raspberry sherbet
1 can (12 ounces) ginger
  ale, chilled

Pour ¼ cup cranberry juice into each of 4 short, fat glasses. Place 1 scoop (about ½ cup) sherbet in each glass. Fill with ginger ale.

Menu #23 (page 69)

MENU 24

CHICKEN CROISSANT SANDWICHES* ◆ SHOESTRING POTATOES ◆ APRICOT FRUIT SALAD*

MENU MAKES 4 SERVINGS

INGREDIENTS

¼ cup pine nuts or slivered almonds

¼ cup apricot preserves or orange marmalade

1 can (1¾ ounces) shoe-string potatoes

1 jar (6 ounces) marinated artichoke hearts

2 tablespoons mayonnaise or salad dressing

4 romaine leaves

1 medium tomato

½ cup alfalfa sprouts

2 cups cut-up fresh fruit

2 packages (3 ounces each) thinly sliced smoked chicken

¼ cup plain yogurt

4 croissants

MENU TIP: Leave the nuts unroasted in the Apricot Fruit Salad—it's equally delicious—or microwave them quickly. Place nuts and 1 teaspoon margarine in microwavable dish. Microwave uncovered on high 1½ to 2 minutes, stirring every 30 seconds, until crisp and golden. Watch carefully!

TIMETABLE

1. Toast pine nuts for Apricot Fruit Salad, if desired.

2. Prepare artichoke mixture for Chicken Croissant Sandwiches.

3. Mix cut-up fruit and preserves for fruit salad.

4. Assemble sandwiches.

5. Sprinkle pine nuts on fruit salad.

NUTRITION INFORMATION PER SERVING

Calories	530	**Percent of U.S. RDA**	
Protein	19	Protein	30
Carbohydrate, grams	55	Vitamin A	26
Fat, grams	28	Vitamin C	26
Cholesterol, milligrams	75	Thiamin	30
Sodium, milligrams	390	Riboflavin	20
Potassium, milligrams	700	Niacin	26
		Calcium	8
		Iron	18

CHICKEN CROISSANT SANDWICHES

1 jar (6 ounces) marinated
    artichoke hearts, drained
1/4 cup plain yogurt
2 tablespoons mayonnaise or
    salad dressing
4 romaine leaves
1 medium tomato, thinly
    sliced
4 croissants, sliced crosswise
2 packages (3 ounces each)
    thinly sliced smoked
    chicken
1/2 cup alfalfa sprouts

Place artichoke hearts, yogurt and mayonnaise in food processor or blender. Cover and process or blend about 15 seconds or until smooth; reserve.

Place 1 romaine leaf and about 2 tomato slices on bottom half of each croissant. Separate slices of chicken and pile about one-fourth of chicken slices on each sandwich. Top with sprouts. Spoon about 2 tablespoons reserved artichoke mixture over each sandwich. Top with remaining croissant halves.

APRICOT FRUIT SALAD

2 cups cut-up fresh fruit
1/4 cup apricot preserves or
    orange marmalade
1/4 cup pine nuts or slivered
    almonds, toasted if desired

Carefully mix cut-up fruit and apricot preserves. Sprinkle with pine nuts.

◇ **MENU 25** ◇

Chicken-Pasta Salad* • Melon Slices • Lemon English Muffins*

MENU MAKES 4 SERVINGS

INGREDIENTS

1 tablespoon honey

1 package (5 ounces) spiral macaroni

⅓ cup mayonnaise or salad dressing

¼ cup French dressing

½ teaspoon grated lemon peel

1 cup cherry tomatoes

½ cantaloupe or honeydew melon

2 cups cut-up cooked chicken (about 12 ounces)

¼ cup (½ stick) margarine or butter

4 English muffins

1 package (6 ounces) frozen pea pods

MENU TIP: Buy chicken already cooked from the meat counter or deli, or use your own leftover cooked chicken. For variety, substitute any salad dressing you have on hand, such as blue cheese, Italian or Caesar, for the French dressing. Using cherry tomatoes also cuts down on the amount of chopping you'll need to do.

TIMETABLE

1. Heat water for macaroni in Chicken-Pasta Salad.

2. Remove pea pods from package; place in bowl of cool water to thaw.

3. Cut up chicken and cherry tomatoes.

4. Cook macaroni and pea pods.

5. Cut melon slices.

6. Prepare Lemon English Muffins.

7. Toss pasta salad.

NUTRITION INFORMATION PER SERVING

		Percent of U.S. RDA	
Calories	720		
Protein, grams	31	Protein	46
Carbohydrate, grams	65	Vitamin A	100
Fat, grams	38	Vitamin C	100
Cholesterol, milligrams	60	Thiamin	24
Sodium, milligrams	710	Riboflavin	18
Potassium, milligrams	800	Niacin	40
		Calcium	10
		Iron	20

CHICKEN-PASTA SALAD

1 package (6 ounces) frozen pea pods
1 package (5 ounces) spiral macaroni
⅓ cup mayonnaise or salad dressing
¼ cup French dressing
2 cups cut-up cooked chicken (about 12 ounces)
1 cup cherry tomatoes, cut into halves

Remove pea pods from package. Place pea pods in bowl of cool water until thawed; drain. Cook macaroni as directed on package—except add pea pods about 2 minutes before macaroni is done; drain. Rinse macaroni and pea pods with cold water; drain. Mix mayonnaise and French dressing in large bowl. Add macaroni mixture and remaining ingredients; toss.

LEMON ENGLISH MUFFINS

4 English muffins, split
¼ cup (½ stick) margarine or butter, softened
1 tablespoon honey
½ teaspoon grated lemon peel

Set oven control to broil. Place muffins, cut sides up, on rack in broiler pan. Broil 4 inches from heat 2 to 3 minutes or until golden brown. Mix margarine, honey and lemon peel. Spread over hot muffins.

**MENU
26**

HOT GERMAN CHICKEN SALAD* • SWISS CHEESE TRIANGLES* • POUND CAKE WITH MAPLE-NUT TOPPING*

MENU MAKES 4 SERVINGS

INGREDIENTS

¼ cup coarsely chopped pecans

1 tablespoon all-purpose flour

¼ cup maple-flavored syrup

2 tablespoons vegetable oil

2 tablespoons white wine vinegar

2 teaspoons Dijon mustard

2 teaspoons chopped fresh or ½ teaspoon dried thyme

¼ teaspoon salt

⅛ teaspoon pepper

Freshly ground pepper

2 medium tomatoes

½ bunch romaine

2 ounces mushrooms

2 green onions

4 skinless boneless chicken breast halves (about 1 pound)

1 cup shredded Swiss cheese (4 ounces)

1 container (4 ounces) whipped light cream cheese (Neufchâtel cheese)

4 slices pound cake

4 slices dark rye bread

MENU TIP: Rinse the romaine and tear into pieces; keep in a towel in the vegetable drawer of the refrigerator for quick salads. By cooking the pea pods for the salad with the pasta, you eliminate a pot.

TIMETABLE

1. Brown chicken for Hot German Chicken Salad.

2. Prepare vegetables for chicken salad.

3. Prepare Swiss Cheese Triangles.

4. Finish chicken while triangles broil.

5. Just before serving, prepare Pound Cake with Maple-Nut Topping.

NUTRITION INFORMATION PER SERVING

		Percent of U.S. RDA	
Calories	580		
Protein, grams	36	Protein	56
Carbohydrate; grams	52	Vitamin A	58
Fat, grams	26	Vitamin C	24
Cholesterol, milligrams	135	Thiamin	22
Sodium, milligrams	550	Riboflavin	22
Potassium, milligrams	850	Niacin	68
		Calcium	12
		Iron	18

HOT GERMAN CHICKEN SALAD

4 skinless boneless chicken
 breast halves (about
 1 pound)
2 tablespoons vegetable oil
1 tablespoon all-purpose flour
¼ teaspoon salt
⅛ teaspoon pepper
½ cup water
2 tablespoons white wine
 vinegar
2 teaspoons Dijon mustard
2 teaspoons chopped fresh or
 ½ teaspoon dried thyme
2 ounces mushrooms, sliced
 (about ¾ cup)
2 green onions (with tops),
 thinly sliced
½ bunch romaine, torn into
 bite-size pieces
2 medium tomatoes, cut into
 wedges

Cook chicken breast halves in oil in 10-inch nonstick skillet over medium heat about 6 minutes on each side or until done. Remove chicken from skillet; drain. Cool chicken slightly and cut into thin slices.

Stir flour, salt and pepper into drippings in skillet. Cook over low heat, stirring constantly, until smooth and bubbly; remove from heat. Stir in water, vinegar, mustard, thyme, mushrooms and green onions. Cook over low heat, stirring constantly, until mixture is bubbly. Cook and stir 1 minute. Divide romaine among 4 salad plates. Arrange chicken and tomatoes on romaine. Spoon mushroom mixture over top.

SWISS CHEESE TRIANGLES

1 cup shredded Swiss cheese
 (4 ounces)
4 slices dark rye bread
Freshly ground pepper

Set oven control to broil. Sprinkle ¼ cup cheese evenly over each slice bread. Sprinkle with pepper. Broil bread with tops about 4 inches from heat 2 to 3 minutes or until cheese is melted. Cut each slice bread into 4 triangles.

POUND CAKE WITH MAPLE-NUT TOPPING

1 container (4 ounces)
 whipped light cream
 cheese (Neufchâtel
 cheese), softened
¼ cup maple-flavored syrup
¼ cup coarsely chopped
 pecans
4 slices pound cake

Mix whipped cream cheese, maple-flavored syrup and pecans. Spoon over pound cake.

MENU
27

CHICKEN AND LEEK SOUP* ◆ QUICK CORN BREAD STICKS* ◆ PINEAPPLE SORBET WITH RASPBERRIES*

MENU MAKES 4 SERVINGS

INGREDIENTS

½ cup variety baking mix

½ cup cornmeal

1 tablespoon vegetable oil

½ cup uncooked quick barley

1 package (1.8 ounces) leek soup and recipe mix

4 tablespoons raspberry-flavored liqueur, if desired

1½ cups cut-up cooked chicken

1 cup milk

¾ cup buttermilk

¼ cup honey butter

1 egg

1 pint pineapple sorbet

1 package (10 ounces) frozen raspberries in syrup

MENU TIP: Purchase frozen cut-up, cooked chicken or cooked chicken from the deli, or use leftover cooked chicken for the soup. Using baking mix is a fast and convenient way to prepare corn bread sticks.

TIMETABLE

1. Heat oven for Quick Corn Bread Sticks.

2. Remove raspberries from freezer for Pineapple Sorbet with Raspberries. Place package in warm water to thaw.

3. Prepare Chicken and Leek Soup.

4. Prepare corn bread sticks.

5. Divide raspberries among dessert dishes.

6. Just before serving, top raspberries with pineapple sorbet and liqueur.

NUTRITION INFORMATION PER SERVING

Calories	575	**Percent of U.S. RDA**	
Protein, grams	23	Protein	36
Carbohydrate, grams	93	Vitamin A	2
Fat, grams	12	Vitamin C	6
Cholesterol, milligrams	100	Thiamin	14
Sodium, milligrams	970	Riboflavin	20
Potassium, milligrams	360	Niacin	26
		Calcium	10
		Iron	14

CHICKEN AND LEEK SOUP

1 package (1.8 ounces) leek
    soup and recipe mix (dry)
½ cup uncooked quick barley
1 cup milk
1½ cups cut-up cooked
    chicken

Prepare soup as directed on package—except add barley and increase milk to 1 cup. Stir chicken in with the milk.

QUICK CORN BREAD STICKS

1 egg
½ cup variety baking mix
½ cup cornmeal
¾ cup buttermilk
1 tablespoon vegetable oil
Cornmeal
¼ cup honey butter

Heat oven to 450°. Spray loaf pan, 9 × 5 × 3 inches, with nonstick cooking spray. Beat egg with hand beater until fluffy. Beat in baking mix, ½ cup cornmeal, the buttermilk and oil just until smooth. (Do not overbeat.)

Pour into pan. Sprinkle lightly with cornmeal. Bake about 15 minutes or until toothpick inserted in center comes out clean. Remove from pan. Cut into 8 sticks. Serve hot with honey butter.

PINEAPPLE SORBET WITH RASPBERRIES

1 package (10 ounces) fro-
    zen raspberries in syrup,
    thawed
1 pint pineapple sorbet
4 tablespoons raspberry-
    flavored liqueur, if desired

Divide raspberries and syrup evenly among 4 dessert dishes. Top with 1 scoop pineapple sorbet and drizzle each with 1 tablespoon liqueur.

Glazed Turkey Tenderloins* • Brown Rice and Onions* • Cut-up Vegetables • Apple Wedges with Amber Sauce*

MENU MAKES 4 SERVINGS

INGREDIENTS

½ cup packed brown sugar

¼ cup light corn syrup

1 tablespoon vegetable oil

1½ cups uncooked instant brown rice

1¼ cups chicken broth

⅓ cup orange marmalade

1 teaspoon Worcestershire sauce

1 teaspoon finely chopped gingerroot or ½ tea-spoon ground ginger

Cut-up vegetables

¼ cup chopped green onion

4 apples

2 turkey breast tenderloins (about 1¼ pounds)

¼ cup half-and-half

3 tablespoons margarine or butter

MENU TIP: Buy fresh vegetables already cut up or keep a supply in refrigerator, cut up and ready to eat. Use an "apple wedger" to cut the apples easily in one motion.

TIMETABLE

1. Prepare Glazed Turkey Tenderloins.

2. Prepare Amber Sauce while turkey is browning.

3. Prepare Brown Rice and Onions while turkey is simmering.

4. Just before serving, cut apples into wedges. Dip wedges into sauce or place in dessert dishes and top with sauce.

NUTRITION INFORMATION PER SERVING

		Percent of U.S. RDA	
Calories	840		
Protein, grams	38	Protein	58
Carbohydrate, grams	120	Vitamin A	100
Fat, grams	25	Vitamin C	32
Cholesterol, milligrams	100	Thiamin	22
Sodium, milligrams	490	Riboflavin	18
Potassium, milligrams	960	Niacin	52
		Calcium	12
		Iron	32

GLAZED TURKEY TENDERLOINS

2 turkey breast tenderloins
   (about 1¼ pounds)
1 tablespoon vegetable oil
⅓ cup orange marmalade
1 teaspoon finely chopped
   gingerroot or ½ teaspoon
   ground ginger
1 teaspoon Worcestershire
   sauce

Cook turkey breast tenderloins in oil in 10-inch skillet over medium heat about 5 minutes or until brown on one side; turn turkey. Stir in remaining ingredients; reduce heat.

Cover and simmer 15 to 20 minutes, stirring occasionally, until turkey is done and sauce is thickened. Cut turkey into thin slices. Spoon sauce over turkey.

BROWN RICE AND ONIONS

1¼ cups chicken broth
¼ cup chopped green onion
1 tablespoon margarine or
   butter
1½ cups uncooked instant
   brown rice

Heat chicken broth, onion and margarine to boiling in 1½-quart saucepan over medium heat. Stir in rice. Heat to boiling; reduce heat. Cover and simmer 5 minutes. Remove from heat; stir. Cover and let stand 5 minutes. Fluff rice lightly with fork.

AMBER SAUCE

½ cup packed brown sugar
¼ cup light corn syrup
¼ cup half-and-half
2 tablespoons margarine or
   butter

Heat all ingredients to rolling boil in 1-quart saucepan over medium heat, stirring frequently.

TURKEY SLICES WITH WALNUTS* • POPPY SEED BISCUIT WEDGES* • BEETS • MIXED GREENS WITH QUICK TARRAGON DRESSING*

MENU MAKES 4 SERVINGS

INGREDIENTS

1 cup plus 3 tablespoons variety baking mix

⅓ cup walnut pieces

1 teaspoon sugar

1 teaspoon cornstarch

1 jar (16 ounces) beets

½ cup dry white wine

⅓ cup mayonnaise or salad dressing

1 teaspoon tarragon vinegar

1 teaspoon poppy seed

¼ teaspoon salt

Freshly ground pepper

4 cups bite-size pieces mixed greens

2 green onions

1 package (16 ounces) uncooked turkey breast slices

3 tablespoons plus 1 teaspoon margarine or butter

2 teaspoons milk

MENU TIP: For quick salads, keep greens washed and wrapped in a towel in the vegetable drawer of the refrigerator. You can prepare Quick Tarragon Dressing the night before to save even more time.

TIMETABLE

1. Heat oven for Poppy Seed Biscuit Wedges.

2. Prepare Quick Tarragon Dressing and salad greens.

3. Prepare Poppy Seed Biscuit Wedges.

4. Prepare Turkey Slices with Walnuts.

5. Prepare beets after removing turkey from skillet.

6. Toss greens and dressing.

NUTRITION INFORMATION PER SERVING

		Percent of U.S. RDA	
Calories	655		
Protein, grams	30	Protein	46
Carbohydrate, grams	33	Vitamin A	18
Fat, grams	42	Vitamin C	4
Cholesterol, milligrams	75	Thiamin	22
Sodium, milligrams	840	Riboflavin	18
Potassium, milligrams	550	Niacin	38
		Calcium	12
		Iron	26

TURKEY SLICES WITH WALNUTS

2 tablespoons margarine or
  butter
1 package (about 16 ounces)
  uncooked turkey breast
  slices
¼ teaspoon salt
1 tablespoon margarine or
  butter
⅓ cup walnut pieces
2 green onions (with tops),
  sliced
1 teaspoon cornstarch
½ cup dry white wine
1 teaspoon sugar

Heat 2 tablespoons margarine in 12-inch skillet over medium-high heat until melted. Sauté turkey slices about 4 minutes or until brown on both sides, sprinkling with salt after turning. Remove from skillet; keep warm. Add 1 tablespoon margarine to skillet. Cook walnuts and green onions in margarine over medium heat 2 to 3 minutes or until onions are soft. Stir cornstarch into wine; pour into skillet. Add sugar. Heat to boiling; boil and stir 1 minute. Pour over turkey slices.

POPPY SEED BISCUIT WEDGES

1 cup plus 3 tablespoons variety baking mix
1 teaspoon poppy seed
⅓ cup cold water
1 teaspoon margarine or butter, softened

Heat oven to 450°. Mix baking mix, poppy seed and water until soft dough forms. Beat vigorously 30 seconds. Turn dough onto ungreased cookie sheet. Dip fingers in baking mix and pat dough into 6-inch circle. Cut into 8 wedges, cutting completely through dough. Brush with margarine. Bake 12 to 15 minutes or until golden brown.

QUICK TARRAGON DRESSING

⅓ cup mayonnaise or salad
  dressing
2 teaspoons milk
1 teaspoon tarragon vinegar
Freshly ground pepper

Mix mayonnaise, milk and vinegar until smooth. Spoon over mixed greens. Sprinkle with freshly ground pepper.

MENU
30

Southwest Turkey Fajitas* • Pickled Peppers • Spicy Jalapeño Mexican Beans • Pineapple Melba*

MENU MAKES 4 SERVINGS

INGREDIENTS

1 tablespoon vegetable oil

1 tablespoon brandy, if desired

1 can (15 ounces) spicy jalapeño Mexican beans

1 jar (10 to 12 ounces) chunky red salsa

1 can (15¼ ounces) spear pineapple

1 can (8 ounces) sliced peaches

4 pickled peppers

1 tablespoon lime juice

¼ teaspoon crushed red pepper

1 clove garlic

½ cup fresh or frozen raspberries

12 ounces cooked turkey

8 flour tortillas (7 inches in diameter)

1 container (6 ounces) frozen guacamole

MENU TIP: The beans and the tortillas can be heated in the microwave—see page 153 for tortilla directions.

TIMETABLE

1. Heat oven to 325° to warm tortillas.

2. Mix lime juice, red pepper, garlic and turkey for Southwest Turkey Fajitas. Cover and refrigerate.

3. Wrap tortillas in foil and place in oven.

4. Prepare Pineapple Melba.

5. Prepare beans.

6. Sauté turkey mixture and assemble fajitas.

NUTRITION INFORMATION PER SERVING

Calories	540	**Percent of U.S. RDA**	
Protein, grams	33	Protein	50
Carbohydrate, grams	67	Vitamin A	26
Fat, grams	17	Vitamin C	30
Cholesterol, milligrams	60	Thiamin	20
Sodium, milligrams	1330	Riboflavin	18
Potassium, milligrams	920	Niacin	34
		Calcium	20
		Iron	44

SOUTHWEST TURKEY FAJITAS

1 tablespoon lime juice
¼ teaspoon crushed red
  pepper
1 clove garlic, crushed
12 ounces cooked turkey, cut
  into about 2-inch strips
  (about 2 cups)
8 flour tortillas (7 inches in
  diameter)
1 tablespoon vegetable oil
1 container (6 ounces) frozen guacamole, thawed
1 jar (10 to 12 ounces)
  chunky red salsa

Heat oven to 325°. Mix lime juice, red pepper and garlic in glass or plastic bowl. Stir in turkey until well coated. Cover and refrigerate.

Wrap tortillas in aluminum foil; heat in oven about 15 minutes or until warm.

Heat oil in wok or 10-inch skillet over medium-high heat. Sauté turkey in oil about 2 minutes, stirring frequently, until turkey is hot.

Divide the turkey and guacamole among the tortillas. Top each with 2 tablespoons salsa. Fold 1 end of tortillas up about 1 inch over turkey mixture; fold right and left sides over folded ends, overlapping. Fold down remaining ends. Serve with remaining salsa.

PINEAPPLE MELBA

1 can (8 ounces) sliced
  peaches, drained
1 can (15¼ ounces) spear
  pineapple, drained
1 tablespoon brandy, if
  desired
½ cup fresh or frozen
  (thawed) raspberries

Place peaches in food processor or blender. Cover and process or blend until smooth. Divide pineapple among 4 dessert dishes. Sprinkle with brandy. Top with puree and raspberries.

Pineapple with Apricot Puree: Substitute 1 can (8 ounces) apricot halves for the peaches and blueberries for the raspberries.

Turkey Patties and Vegetables* ♦ Italian Bread with Herb Spread* ♦ Fresh Pears

MENU MAKES 4 SERVINGS

INGREDIENTS

¼ cup dry bread crumbs

1 tablespoon olive oil

1 tablespoon lemon juice

1 teaspoon salt

1 teaspoon rubbed sage

¼ teaspoon pepper

¼ teaspoon Italian seasoning

2 medium zucchini

1 medium red bell pepper

1 medium onion

4 pears

1 pound ground turkey

3 tablespoons margarine or butter

1 tablespoon grated Parmesan cheese

4 slices Italian bread

MENU TIP: First, shape the turkey patties and then cut up the zucchini, bell pepper and onion while they're browning.

TIMETABLE

1. Shape turkey patties for Turkey Patties and Vegetables; begin browning.

2. Cut vegetables for turkey patties; add to skillet.

3. Prepare Italian Bread with Herb Spread.

NUTRITION INFORMATION PER SERVING

		Percent of U.S. RDA	
Calories	490		
Protein, grams	31	Protein	48
Carbohydrate, grams	55	Vitamin A	20
Fat, grams	17	Vitamin C	50
Cholesterol, milligrams	75	Thiamin	20
Sodium, milligrams	970	Riboflavin	24
Potassium, milligrams	910	Niacin	34
		Calcium	8
		Iron	22

TURKEY PATTIES AND VEGETABLES

1 pound ground turkey
¼ cup dry bread crumbs
1 tablespoon lemon juice
1 tablespoon olive oil
1 teaspoon salt
1 teaspoon rubbed sage
¼ teaspoon pepper
1 tablespoon margarine or
    butter
2 medium zucchini, cut into
    1-inch pieces
1 medium red bell pepper,
    cut into 1½-inch pieces
1 medium onion, cut into
    8 wedges

Mix ground turkey, bread crumbs, lemon juice, oil, salt, sage and pepper. Shape mixture into 4 patties, each about ½ inch thick. Heat margarine in 10-inch skillet over medium heat until melted. Cook patties in margarine, turning once, until brown on both sides. Add remaining ingredients. Cover and cook about 9 minutes or until turkey is done and vegetables are crisp-tender.

ITALIAN BREAD WITH HERB SPREAD

4 slices Italian bread
2 tablespoons margarine or
    butter, softened
1 tablespoon grated
    Parmesan cheese
¼ teaspoon Italian seasoning

Set oven control to broil. Place bread on rack in broiler pan and broil about 4 inches from heat about 2 minutes or until brown. Mix remaining ingredients. Spread over untoasted sides of bread. Broil about 1½ minutes or until hot and bubbly. Cut each slice into 3 strips.

◆ MENU 32 ◆

Turkey Oven Sandwich* ◆ Dill Pickle Spears ◆ Pickled Baby Corn ◆ Fruit and Yogurt*

MENU MAKES 4 SERVINGS

MENU TIP: These delicious hot sandwiches incorporate bread, vegetables and meat into one dish so you don't spend time preparing separate dishes. Add purchased pickles for an easy condiment.

INGREDIENTS

- 1 tablespoon packed brown sugar
- ⅓ cup mayonnaise or salad dressing
- 4 dill pickle spears
- 4 ears pickled baby corn
- Chocolate-flavored syrup, if desired
- ½ teaspoon poultry seasoning
- Paprika, if desired
- 1 medium tomato
- 1 stalk celery
- 1 tablespoon chopped onion
- 1 medium pear
- 1 cup seedless grapes
- 1 kiwifruit
- 1 pound ground turkey
- ½ cup sour cream
- ½ cup shredded sharp Cheddar cheese (2 ounces)
- ¼ cup plain yogurt
- 1 tablespoon margarine or butter
- 2 pita breads (6 inches in diameter)

TIMETABLE

1. Prepare Turkey Oven Sandwich.

2. Prepare Fruit and Yogurt while sandwiches are baking.

NUTRITION INFORMATION PER SERVING

		Percent of U.S. RDA	
Calories	615		
Protein, grams	34	Protein	52
Carbohydrate, grams	47	Vitamin A	22
Fat, grams	32	Vitamin C	40
Cholesterol, milligrams	105	Thiamin	12
Sodium, milligrams	820	Riboflavin	22
Potassium, milligrams	860	Niacin	30
		Calcium	20
		Iron	16

TURKEY OVEN SANDWICH

1 pound ground turkey
1 tablespoon margarine or
butter
½ teaspoon poultry
seasoning
2 pita breads (6 inches in
diameter), cut in half
1 medium tomato, thinly
sliced
1 stalk celery, sliced
½ cup shredded sharp Ched-
dar cheese (2 ounces)
½ cup sour cream
⅓ cup mayonnaise or salad
dressing
1 tablespoon chopped onion
Paprika, if desired

Heat oven to 425°. Cook and stir ground turkey, margarine and poultry seasoning in 10-inch skillet, over medium heat, until turkey is done; drain. Place pita breads on bottom and about halfway up sides of ungreased square pan, 9 × 9 × 2 inches, (they will overlap slightly in middle). Layer turkey, tomato and celery on pitas. Mix remaining ingredients except paprika; spoon over top. Sprinkle with paprika. Bake 12 to 15 minutes or until topping is light brown.

FRUIT AND YOGURT

1 tablespoon packed brown
sugar
¼ cup plain yogurt
1 cup seedless grapes
1 medium pear, sliced
1 kiwifruit, pared and sliced
Chocolate-flavored syrup, if
desired

Mix brown sugar and yogurt. Divide grapes, pear and kiwifruit among 4 dessert dishes. Top fruit in each dish with about 1 tablespoon yogurt mixture. Drizzle with syrup.

◇
**MENU
33**

TURKEY SALAD WITH HONEY ALMONDS* ◆ SLICED TOMATOES WITH BALSAMIC VINEGAR ◆ PARMESAN-RYE FINGERS*

MENU MAKES 4 SERVINGS

INGREDIENTS

½ cup honey-roasted almonds

2 tablespoons honey

1 tablespoon balsamic or red wine vinegar

1 teaspoon lemon juice

1 tablespoon chopped fresh parsley or 1 teaspoon parsley flakes

1 teaspoon dry mustard

2 medium stalks celery

2 medium tomatoes

2 tart red apples

8 ounces sliced cooked turkey

4 ounces provolone or Swiss cheese

½ cup sour cream or plain yogurt

2 tablespoons margarine or butter

2 tablespoons grated Parmesan cheese

4 slices rye bread with caraway seed

MENU TIP: Leftover cooked turkey is perfect for this salad, or use sliced turkey from the deli.

TIMETABLE

1. Prepare Turkey Salad with Honey Almonds.

2. Set oven control to broil.

3. Slice tomatoes and sprinkle with vinegar.

4. Prepare Parmesan-Rye Fingers.

NUTRITION INFORMATION PER SERVING

Calories	585	**Percent of U.S. RDA**	
Protein, grams	33	Protein	50
Carbohydrate, grams	44	Vitamin A	30
Fat, grams	33	Vitamin C	20
Cholesterol, milligrams	85	Thiamin	12
Sodium, milligrams	540	Riboflavin	26
Potassium, milligrams	790	Niacin	22
		Calcium	44
		Iron	16

TURKEY SALAD WITH HONEY ALMONDS

Honey Dressing (below)
½ cup honey-roasted almonds
8 ounces sliced cooked turkey, cut into ¼-inch strips (about 2 cups)
4 ounces provolone or Swiss cheese, cut into cubes
2 medium stalks celery, sliced
2 unpared tart red apples, cut into cubes
Honey-roasted almonds, if desired

½ cup sour cream or plain yogurt
2 tablespoons honey
1 tablespoon chopped fresh parsley or 1 teaspoon parsley flakes
1 teaspoon dry mustard
1 teaspoon lemon juice

Prepare Honey Dressing. Add remaining ingredients to bowl; toss. Sprinkle with additional honey-roasted almonds.

Honey Dressing

Mix all ingredients in large bowl.

PARMESAN-RYE FINGERS

4 slices rye bread with caraway seed
2 tablespoons margarine or butter, softened
2 tablespoons grated Parmesan cheese

Set oven control to broil. Spread each slice of bread with margarine. Sprinkle with Parmesan cheese. Cut each slice crosswise into 4 strips and place on rack in broiler pan. Broil 4 inches from heat 1½ to 2 minutes or until cheese is brown.

Menu #44 (page 125)

CHAPTER 4
FISH AND
SHELLFISH

◆ MENU
34 ◆

POACHED RED SNAPPER* ◆ CREAMY TOMATO SAUCE* ◆ CURRIED PEAS AND RICE*

MENU MAKES 4 SERVINGS

INGREDIENTS

1½ cups uncooked instant rice

2 tablespoons sliced almonds

1 tablespoon tomato paste

½ cup mayonnaise or salad dressing

½ cup dry white wine or water

1½ teaspoons chopped fresh or ½ teaspoon dried oregano

1 teaspoon curry powder

½ teaspoon salt

2 tablespoons chopped shallots or onion

1 jalapeño chili

½ medium tomato

1 small lime

1 pound red snapper fillets

1 tablespoon margarine or butter

1½ cups frozen green peas

MENU TIP: Keeping a tube of tomato paste in the refrigerator is great when you need small amounts, as in Creamy Tomato Sauce. By cooking the peas in the same water as the rice, you'll dovetail and save time—and you'll have one pot fewer to wash.

TIMETABLE

1. Prepare Creamy Tomato Sauce.

2. Start poaching liquid for Poached Red Snapper.

3. Heat peas to boiling for Curried Peas and Rice.

4. Add fish to poaching liquid.

5. Stir rice, then almonds, into peas.

NUTRITION INFORMATION PER SERVING

		Percent of U.S. RDA	
Calories	735		
Protein, grams	33	Protein	50
Carbohydrate, grams	81	Vitamin A	8
Fat, grams	28	Vitamin C	16
Cholesterol, milligrams	40	Thiamin	34
Sodium, milligrams	570	Riboflavin	2
Potassium, milligrams	650	Niacin	20
		Calcium	6
		Iron	22

TURKEY OVEN SANDWICH

1 pound ground turkey
1 tablespoon margarine or
    butter
½ teaspoon poultry
    seasoning
2 pita breads (6 inches in
    diameter), cut in half
1 medium tomato, thinly
    sliced
1 stalk celery, sliced
½ cup shredded sharp Ched-
    dar cheese (2 ounces)
½ cup sour cream
⅓ cup mayonnaise or salad
    dressing
1 tablespoon chopped onion
Paprika, if desired

Heat oven to 425°. Cook and stir ground turkey, margarine and poultry seasoning in 10-inch skillet, over medium heat, until turkey is done; drain. Place pita breads on bottom and about halfway up sides of ungreased square pan, 9 × 9 × 2 inches, (they will overlap slightly in middle). Layer turkey, tomato and celery on pitas. Mix remaining ingredients except paprika; spoon over top. Sprinkle with paprika. Bake 12 to 15 minutes or until topping is light brown.

FRUIT AND YOGURT

1 tablespoon packed brown
    sugar
¼ cup plain yogurt
1 cup seedless grapes
1 medium pear, sliced
1 kiwifruit, pared and sliced
Chocolate-flavored syrup, if
    desired

Mix brown sugar and yogurt. Divide grapes, pear and kiwifruit among 4 dessert dishes. Top fruit in each dish with about 1 tablespoon yogurt mixture. Drizzle with syrup.

Menu #32 (page 91)

TURKEY SALAD WITH HONEY ALMONDS* ◆ SLICED TOMATOES WITH BALSAMIC VINEGAR ◆ PARMESAN-RYE FINGERS*

MENU MAKES 4 SERVINGS

INGREDIENTS

½ cup honey-roasted almonds

2 tablespoons honey

1 tablespoon balsamic or red wine vinegar

1 teaspoon lemon juice

1 tablespoon chopped fresh parsley or 1 teaspoon parsley flakes

1 teaspoon dry mustard

2 medium stalks celery

2 medium tomatoes

2 tart red apples

8 ounces sliced cooked turkey

4 ounces provolone or Swiss cheese

½ cup sour cream or plain yogurt

2 tablespoons margarine or butter

2 tablespoons grated Parmesan cheese

4 slices rye bread with caraway seed

MENU TIP: Leftover cooked turkey is perfect for this salad, or use sliced turkey from the deli.

TIMETABLE

1. Prepare Turkey Salad with Honey Almonds.

2. Set oven control to broil.

3. Slice tomatoes and sprinkle with vinegar.

4. Prepare Parmesan-Rye Fingers.

NUTRITION INFORMATION PER SERVING

		Percent of U.S. RDA	
Calories	585		
Protein, grams	33	Protein	50
Carbohydrate, grams	44	Vitamin A	30
Fat, grams	33	Vitamin C	20
Cholesterol, milligrams	85	Thiamin	12
Sodium, milligrams	540	Riboflavin	26
Potassium, milligrams	790	Niacin	22
		Calcium	44
		Iron	16

TURKEY SALAD WITH HONEY ALMONDS

Honey Dressing (below)
½ cup honey-roasted almonds
8 ounces sliced cooked turkey, cut into ¼-inch strips (about 2 cups)
4 ounces provolone or Swiss cheese, cut into cubes
2 medium stalks celery, sliced
2 unpared tart red apples, cut into cubes
Honey-roasted almonds, if desired

½ cup sour cream or plain yogurt
2 tablespoons honey
1 tablespoon chopped fresh parsley or 1 teaspoon parsley flakes
1 teaspoon dry mustard
1 teaspoon lemon juice

Prepare Honey Dressing. Add remaining ingredients to bowl; toss. Sprinkle with additional honey-roasted almonds.

Honey Dressing

Mix all ingredients in large bowl.

PARMESAN-RYE FINGERS

*4 slices rye bread with car-
away seed*
*2 tablespoons margarine or
butter, softened*
*2 tablespoons grated
Parmesan cheese*

Set oven control to broil. Spread each slice of bread with margarine. Sprinkle with Parmesan cheese. Cut each slice crosswise into 4 strips and place on rack in broiler pan. Broil 4 inches from heat 1½ to 2 minutes or until cheese is brown.

Menu #44 (page 125)

CHAPTER 4
FISH AND SHELLFISH

MENU
34

POACHED RED SNAPPER* • CREAMY TOMATO SAUCE* • CURRIED PEAS AND RICE*

MENU MAKES 4 SERVINGS

INGREDIENTS

1½ cups uncooked instant rice

2 tablespoons sliced almonds

1 tablespoon tomato paste

½ cup mayonnaise or salad dressing

½ cup dry white wine or water

1½ teaspoons chopped fresh or ½ teaspoon dried oregano

1 teaspoon curry powder

½ teaspoon salt

2 tablespoons chopped shallots or onion

1 jalapeño chili

½ medium tomato

1 small lime

1 pound red snapper fillets

1 tablespoon margarine or butter

1½ cups frozen green peas

MENU TIP: Keeping a tube of tomato paste in the refrigerator is great when you need small amounts, as in Creamy Tomato Sauce. By cooking the peas in the same water as the rice, you'll dovetail and save time—and you'll have one pot fewer to wash.

TIMETABLE

1. Prepare Creamy Tomato Sauce.

2. Start poaching liquid for Poached Red Snapper.

3. Heat peas to boiling for Curried Peas and Rice.

4. Add fish to poaching liquid.

5. Stir rice, then almonds, into peas.

NUTRITION INFORMATION PER SERVING

Calories	735	**Percent of U.S. RDA**	
Protein, grams	33	Protein	50
Carbohydrate, grams	81	Vitamin A	8
Fat, grams	28	Vitamin C	16
Cholesterol, milligrams	40	Thiamin	34
Sodium, milligrams	570	Riboflavin	2
Potassium, milligrams	650	Niacin	20
		Calcium	6
		Iron	22

POACHED RED SNAPPER

½ cup dry white wine or water

2 tablespoons chopped shallots or onion

1 small lime, sliced

1 jalapeño chili, sliced into rings

1 pound red snapper fillets, cut into serving pieces

Stir wine, shallots, lime and chili in 12-inch skillet. Add red snapper. Add enough water to cover fillets. Heat to a simmer over low heat. Cook fillets 8 to 10 minutes or until fish flakes easily with fork. Carefully remove fillets from liquid; drain. Serve with Creamy Tomato Sauce.

CREAMY TOMATO SAUCE

½ cup mayonnaise or salad dressing

1 tablespoon tomato paste

½ medium tomato, chopped (¼ cup)

¼ cup chopped tomato

1½ teaspoons chopped fresh or ½ teaspoon dried oregano

Mix all ingredients. Cover and refrigerate until ready to serve.

CURRIED PEAS AND RICE

1½ cups frozen green peas

1½ cups water

1 tablespoon margarine or butter

½ teaspoon salt

½ to 1 teaspoon curry powder

1½ cups uncooked instant rice

2 tablespoons sliced almonds

Heat peas, water, margarine, salt and curry powder to boiling in 2-quart saucepan. Stir in rice. Remove from heat and cover. Let stand 5 minutes. Stir in almonds, fluffing rice.

MENU
35

SAVORY BROILED COD* • CUT ASPARAGUS • ALMOND-ORANGE SALAD*

MENU MAKES 4 SERVINGS

INGREDIENTS

1 tablespoon sugar

2 tablespoons vegetable oil

2 tablespoons sliced almonds

½ can (11-ounce size) mandarin orange segments

¼ cup mayonnaise or salad dressing

1 tablespoon vinegar

2 teaspoons prepared horseradish

¼ cup chopped fresh parsley

¼ teaspoon salt

Dash of pepper

2 cups cut asparagus

¾ cup chopped celery

3 green onions

1½ heads Bibb lettuce

1 pound cod or other firm lean fish fillets (about ¾ inch thick)

MENU TIP: Do all of the chopping and slicing at one time while you are at the chopping board. Chop ¼ cup of parsley and divide it in half for the salad dressing and fish.

TIMETABLE

1. Prepare dressing for Almond-Orange Salad.

2. Prepare cod from Savory Broiled Cod for broiling.

3. Prepare asparagus.

4. Broil cod; mix remaining ingredients.

5. Toss salad.

6. Spread cod with topping.

NUTRITION INFORMATION PER SERVING

Calories	540	**Percent of U.S. RDA**	
Protein, grams	38	Protein	58
Carbohydrate, grams	15	Vitamin A	52
Fat, grams	37	Vitamin C	42
Cholesterol, milligrams	55	Thiamin	22
Sodium, milligrams	440	Riboflavin	22
Potassium, milligrams	1110	Niacin	24
		Calcium	12
		Iron	18

SAVORY BROILED COD

1 pound cod or other firm
lean fish fillets (about
¾ inch thick)
¼ cup mayonnaise or salad
dressing
2 tablespoons chopped fresh
parsley
2 teaspoons prepared
horseradish
2 green onions (with tops),
finely chopped

Set oven control to broil. Grease rack in broiler pan. Place cod on rack. Broil 4 inches from heat 8 minutes. Mix remaining ingredients in small bowl. Spread on fish. Broil 1 to 2 minutes or until topping is light brown and fish flakes easily with fork.

ALMOND-ORANGE SALAD

Dressing (below)
2 cups bite-size pieces Bibb
lettuce (about 1½ heads)
¾ cup chopped celery
1 green onion, thinly sliced
½ can (11-ounce size) mandarin orange segments,
drained
2 tablespoons sliced almonds

1 tablespoon sugar
2 tablespoons vegetable oil
1 tablespoon vinegar
¼ teaspoon salt
Dash of pepper

Prepare Dressing; reserve. Mix remaining ingredients in salad bowl. Toss with Dressing.

Dressing
Shake all ingredients in tightly covered container.

GRILLED GARLIC HALIBUT* ◆ CUT GREEN BEANS WITH GARLIC SAUCE* ◆ GRILLED TEXAS TOAST*

MENU MAKES 4 SERVINGS

INGREDIENTS

⅔ cup olive oil

¼ cup lemon juice

2 tablespoons chopped fresh parsley

½ teaspoon salt

½ teaspoon seasoned salt

⅛ teaspoon ground red pepper (cayenne)

6 cloves garlic

Fresh cilantro, if desired

2 cups cut green beans

4 halibut steaks, 1 inch thick (about 1½ pounds)

¼ cup (½ stick) margarine or butter

4 slices thick-cut white bread, about 1 inch thick

MENU TIP: Using the Garlic Sauce for both the halibut and green beans is an easy way to dress up two dishes and carry the flavor throughout the meal. Chop the garlic for the sauce and fish at one time, or use chopped garlic in oil.

TIMETABLE

1. If using charcoal grill, start coals before meal preparation.

2. Mix oil, salt, pepper and garlic for Grilled Garlic Halibut; spread over fish.

3. Prepare Garlic Sauce.

4. Prepare green beans.

5. Grill fish.

6. Prepare Grilled Texas Toast.

NUTRITION INFORMATION PER SERVING

		Percent of U.S. RDA	
Calories	690		
Protein, grams	40	Protein	62
Carbohydrate, grams	27	Vitamin A	16
Fat, grams	47	Vitamin C	12
Cholesterol, milligrams	55	Thiamin	14
Sodium, milligrams	660	Riboflavin	10
Potassium, milligrams	970	Niacin	10
		Calcium	8
		Iron	12

GRILLED GARLIC HALIBUT

2 tablespoons olive oil
¼ teaspoon salt
⅛ teaspoon ground red pepper (cayenne)
1 clove garlic, finely chopped
4 halibut steaks, 1 inch thick (about 1½ pounds)
Chopped fresh cilantro, if desired

Mix oil, salt, red pepper and garlic; spread on both sides of halibut steaks. Cover and grill on oiled grill 4 inches from medium coals 10 to 15 minutes or until fish flakes easily with fork. Sprinkle with cilantro.

GARLIC SAUCE

5 cloves garlic, coarsely chopped
¼ cup lemon juice
2 tablespoons chopped fresh parsley
¼ teaspoon salt
½ cup olive oil

Place all ingredients except oil in food processor or blender; process until smooth. Slowly add oil while motor is running. Process or blend until mixture is slightly thickened. Serve over Grilled Garlic Halibut and green beans.

GRILLED TEXAS TOAST

¼ cup (½ stick) margarine or butter, softened
4 slices thick-cut white bread, about 1 inch thick
½ teaspoon seasoned salt

Spread margarine on both sides of bread slices. Sprinkle with seasoned salt. Grill bread 4 inches from medium coals 4 to 6 minutes, turning once, until golden brown.

MENU
37

CORNMEAL-FRIED CATFISH* • FRUITY COLESLAW* • CORN MUFFINS • PECAN BUTTER*

MENU MAKES 4 SERVINGS

MENU TIP: Cornmeal muffins and creamy coleslaw can both be purchased at the supermarket, and the Pecan Butter adds pizzazz to both the fish and muffins.

INGREDIENTS

¾ cup cornmeal

¼ cup all-purpose flour

1 tablespoon honey

2 tablespoons vegetable oil

Vegetable oil for frying

½ cup pecans

¼ cup diced dried fruit and raisin mixture

1 tablespoon packed fresh parsley

¼ teaspoon salt

⅛ teaspoon red pepper sauce

6 stems fresh chives

4 catfish fillets (about 1 pound)

½ cup milk

½ cup (1 stick) margarine or butter

2 eggs

4 corn muffins

1 pint creamy coleslaw

TIMETABLE

1. Heat oil.

2. Prepare Fruity Coleslaw. Cover and refrigerate.

3. Prepare Pecan Butter. Cover and refrigerate.

4. Prepare Cornmeal-fried Catfish.

NUTRITION INFORMATION PER SERVING

		Percent of U.S. RDA	
Calories	1010		
Protein, grams	32	Protein	48
Carbohydrate, grams	48	Vitamin A	32
Fat, grams	78	Vitamin C	14
Cholesterol, milligrams	225	Thiamin	26
Sodium, milligrams	1030	Riboflavin	28
Potassium, milligrams	750	Niacin	20
		Calcium	18
		Iron	18

Cornmeal-fried Catfish

Vegetable oil
4 catfish fillets (about
   4 ounces each)
¾ cup cornmeal
¼ cup all-purpose flour
¼ teaspoon salt
½ cup milk
2 eggs, beaten
⅛ teaspoon red pepper sauce
2 tablespoons vegetable oil

Heat oil (2 to 3 inches) in Dutch oven to 375°. Rinse catfish fillets and pat dry. Refrigerate until ready to use.

Mix cornmeal, flour and salt in large bowl. Stir in milk, eggs, pepper sauce and 2 tablespoons vegetable oil until well blended.

Coat fish with cornmeal batter, shaking off any excess. Fry fish in batches 5 to 8 minutes or until golden brown. Drain on paper towels. Keep warm in 275° oven.

Fruity Coleslaw

1 pint creamy coleslaw
¼ cup diced dried fruit and
   raisin mixture
1 tablespoon honey

Drain coleslaw. Mix with fruit bits and honey.

Pecan Butter

½ cup (1 stick) margarine
   or butter, softened
½ cup pecans
1 tablespoon packed fresh
   parsley
6 stems fresh chives, cut into
   1-inch pieces

Place all ingredients in food processor or blender; process until well blended. Serve with Cornmeal-fried Catfish and corn muffins.

◆ **Menu 38**

CHEESE-FISH BURGERS* ◆ DIJON TARTAR SAUCE* ◆ CUT-UP VEGETABLES ◆ CHOCOLATE CHIP COOKIES

INGREDIENTS

½ cup dry bread crumbs

½ cup mayonnaise or salad dressing

2 tablespoons sweet relish

1 tablespoon plus 1 teaspoon lemon juice

½ teaspoon Dijon mustard

2 teaspoons chopped fresh parsley

½ teaspoon salt

¼ teaspoon pepper

1 pound mixed fresh cut-up vegetables

4 lettuce leaves

2 green onions

1 medium tomato

¾ pound cooked orange roughy or other lean fish

2 tablespoons margarine or butter

4 slices process American cheese

2 eggs

4 hamburger buns, if desired

8 chocolate chip cookies

MENU TIP: This menu calls for cooked fish, a great way to use leftover fish from another meal. Or poach, bake or broil fish up to 2 days before serving and store covered in the refrigerator. Purchase precut vegetables in the produce section of the market or at the salad bar. The extra Dijon Tartar Sauce makes a great dip for the vegetables.

TIMETABLE

1. Prepare and cook Cheese-Fish Burgers.

2. Prepare Dijon Tartar Sauce.

3. Arrange vegetables on serving plate.

4. Assemble fish burgers.

NUTRITION INFORMATION PER SERVING

			Percent of U.S. RDA	
Calories		770		
Protein, grams		33	Protein	50
Carbohydrates, grams		45	Vitamin A	100
Fat, grams		51	Vitamin C	42
Cholesterol, milligrams,		205	Thiamin	20
Sodium, milligrams		1490	Riboflavin	30
Potassium, milligrams		910	Niacin	14
			Calcium	42
			Iron	26

CHEESE-FISH BURGERS

¾ pound cooked orange
   roughy or other lean fish
½ cup dry bread crumbs
2 green onions (with tops),
   chopped (about ¼ cup)
1 tablespoon lemon juice
½ teaspoon salt
¼ teaspoon pepper
2 eggs, slightly beaten
2 tablespoons margarine or
   butter
4 slices process American
   cheese
4 hamburger buns, toasted,
   if desired
Dijon Tartar Sauce (below)
1 medium tomato, sliced
4 lettuce leaves

Flake orange roughy. Mix orange roughy, cracker crumbs, green onions, lemon juice, salt, pepper and eggs. Shape into 4 patties, each about ½ inch thick.

Heat margarine in 10-inch skillet over medium heat until melted. Cook patties in margarine about 5 minutes on each side or until golden brown. Top patties with cheese slices during last minute of cooking.

Spread each of 4 bun halves with Dijon Tartar Sauce. Top each with fish patty, tomato, lettuce and remaining bun half.

DIJON TARTAR SAUCE

½ cup mayonnaise or salad
   dressing
2 tablespoons sweet relish
2 teaspoons chopped fresh
   parsley
1 teaspoon lemon juice
½ teaspoon Dijon mustard

Mix all ingredients. Serve with Cheese-Fish Burgers and vegetables.

Menu
39

PESTO-TUNA MELTS* • FRUIT WITH YOGURT SAUCE* • CRANBERRY FIZZ*

MENU MAKES 4 SERVINGS

INGREDIENTS

2 cups ginger ale

2 cups cranberry juice cocktail

2 tablespoons honey

Aromatic bitters, if desired

2 cans (6½ ounces each) tuna

½ cup pesto

1 tablespoon plus 2 teaspoons lemon juice

Freshly ground pepper

2 medium tomatoes

4 cups cut-up fresh fruit

½ cup plain yogurt

4 slices mozzarella cheese (about 6 ounces)

4 slices Italian bread, 1 inch thick

MENU TIP: Buy cut-up fruit in the produce section for all or part of the fruit. Fresh berries, which usually do not need cutting, can be combined quickly with cut-up apples and bananas. A 29-ounce can of peach halves, drained, can be substituted for the fresh fruit.

TIMETABLE

1. Set oven control to broil.

2. Mix yogurt, honey, lemon juice and bitters from Fruit with Yogurt Sauce; cover and refrigerate.

3. Prepare Cranberry Fizz; do not pour over ice.

4. Prepare Pesto-Tuna Melts.

5. Arrange fruit in dishes; drizzle with yogurt sauce.

6. Pour fizz over ice.

NUTRITION INFORMATION PER SERVING

Calories	795	**Percent of U.S. RDA**	
Protein, grams	38	Protein	58
Carbohydrate, grams	84	Vitamin A	38
Fat, grams	36	Vitamin C	100
Cholesterol, milligrams	90	Thiamin	16
Sodium, milligrams	1060	Riboflavin	26
Potassium, milligrams	970	Niacin	54
		Calcium	46
		Iron	30

PESTO-TUNA MELTS

4 slices Italian bread, 1 inch
  thick
½ cup pesto
2 medium tomatoes, thinly
  sliced
2 cans (6½ ounces each)
  tuna, drained
4 slices mozzarella cheese
  (about 6 ounces), cut in
  half
Freshly ground pepper to
  taste

Set oven control to broil. Place bread on ungreased cookie sheet. Broil with tops about 4 inches from heat until golden brown; turn and broil until golden brown. Spread bread slices with pesto. Top with tomato, tuna and cheese slices. Broil about 1 minute or just until cheese begins to melt. Sprinkle with pepper.

FRUIT WITH YOGURT SAUCE

½ cup plain yogurt
2 tablespoons honey
2 teaspoons lemon juice
Dash of aromatic bitters, if
  desired
4 cups cut-up fresh fruit

Mix yogurt, honey, lemon juice and bitters. Divide fruit among 4 serving dishes. Drizzle with yogurt sauce.

CRANBERRY FIZZ

2 cups chilled cranberry juice
  cocktail
2 cups chilled ginger ale
1 tablespoon lemon juice

Mix all ingredients; serve over ice.

TUNA POOR BOYS* ◆ GRAPES AND SOUR CREAM*

MENU MAKES 4 SERVINGS

INGREDIENTS

2 tablespoons olive or vegetable oil

2 tablespoons granulated sugar

4 teaspoons packed brown sugar

2 cans (6½ ounces each) tuna

1 tablespoon chopped fresh or 1 teaspoon dried basil

1 tablespoon chopped fresh parsley

4 lettuce leaves

2 medium tomatoes

1 small onion

3 cups seedless green or red grapes (about ¾ pound)

½ cup sour cream or plain yogurt

2 tablespoons margarine or butter

1 loaf French bread (1 pound)

MENU TIP: This hardy sandwich is a meal in itself, eliminating the need to prepare a salad or soup. Making one large sandwich and cutting it into 4 servings is faster and easier than assembling 4 individual sandwiches.

TIMETABLE

1. Mix sour cream and granulated sugar for Grapes and Sour Cream. Cover and refrigerate.

2. Prepare Tuna Poor Boys.

3. Assemble Grapes and Sour Cream.

NUTRITION INFORMATION PER SERVING

Calories	790	**Percent of U.S. RDA**	
Protein, grams	32	Protein	50
Carbohydrate, grams	104	Vitamin A	30
Fat, grams	28	Vitamin C	34
Cholesterol, milligrams	55	Thiamin	34
Sodium, milligrams	1290	Riboflavin	28
Potassium, milligrams	820	Niacin	58
		Calcium	12
		Iron	28

TUNA POOR BOYS

1 loaf French bread
  (1 pound)
2 tablespoons olive or vegetable oil
2 cans (6½ ounces each)
  tuna, drained and flaked
2 medium tomatoes, sliced
1 small onion, thinly sliced
  and separated into rings
1 tablespoon chopped fresh
  or 1 teaspoon dried basil
1 tablespoon chopped fresh
  parsley
4 lettuce leaves
2 tablespoons margarine or
  butter, softened

Cut bread horizontally in half. Drizzle 1 tablespoon of the oil over bottom half of bread; cover evenly with tuna. Arrange tomatoes and onions over tuna. Drizzle with remaining oil and sprinkle with herbs. Top with lettuce. Spread margarine on remaining bread half. Place on top of sandwich. Secure loaf with wooden picks. Cut into 4 pieces.

GRAPES AND SOUR CREAM

½ cup sour cream or plain
  yogurt
2 tablespoons granulated
  sugar
3 cups seedless green or red
  grapes
4 teaspoons packed brown
  sugar

Mix sour cream and granulated sugar. Divide grapes among 4 dessert dishes. Spoon sour cream mixture evenly over grapes. Sprinkle with brown sugar.

Menu #41 (page 118)

◇ MENU 41 ◇

DILLED PASTA SALAD WITH SMOKED FISH* ◆ BAGEL STICKS ◆ POUND CAKE AND RASPBERRIES WITH RASPBERRY-CHOCOLATE SAUCE*

MENU MAKES 4 SERVINGS

INGREDIENTS

1 package (6 ounces) semi-sweet chocolate chips (1 cup)

¼ cup sugar

1 tablespoon raspberry-flavored liqueur

2 cups uncooked rotini or spiral macaroni (about 6 ounces)

1 can (2¼ ounces) sliced pitted ripe olives

½ cup mayonnaise or salad dressing

1 tablespoon chopped fresh or ½ teaspoon dried dill weed

¼ teaspoon salt

½ teaspoon dry mustard

¼ teaspoon pepper

2 green onions

1 medium zucchini

1 medium carrot

½ pint fresh raspberries

⅔ pound boneless smoked whitefish or salmon (about 2 cups flaked)

¼ cup half-and-half or milk

¼ cup plain yogurt or sour cream

4 slices pound cake

4 bagel sticks

MENU TIP: Rinsing the cooked pasta in cold water is a quick way to make a pasta salad without having to refrigerate the mixture until chilled. Buy frozen or bakery pound cake as the basis of a quick, yet elegant, dessert.

TIMETABLE

1. Defrost frozen pound cake if necessary.

2. Cook pasta for Dilled Pasta Salad with Smoked Fish.

3. Prepare Raspberry-Chocolate Sauce.

4. Assemble pasta salad.

5. Assemble pound cake desserts; reheat chocolate sauce, if desired.

NUTRITION INFORMATION PER SERVING

		Percent of U.S. RDA	
Calories	1105		
Protein, grams	31	Protein	46
Carbohydrate, grams	126	Vitamin A	100
Fat, grams	53	Vitamin C	22
Cholesterol, milligrams	125	Thiamin	50
Sodium, milligrams	1170	Riboflavin	30
Potassium, milligrams	950	Niacin	30
		Calcium	12
		Iron	32

DILLED PASTA SALAD WITH SMOKED FISH

2 cups uncooked rotini or
  spiral macaroni
½ cup mayonnaise or salad
  dressing
¼ cup plain yogurt or sour
  cream
1 tablespoon chopped fresh
  or ½ teaspoon dried dill
  weed
½ teaspoon dry mustard
¼ teaspoon salt
¼ teaspoon pepper
1 can (2¼ ounces) sliced pitted ripe olives, drained
  (about ½ cup)
2 green onions (with tops),
  thinly sliced
1 medium zucchini, thinly
  sliced (about 2 cups)
1 medium carrot, thinly
  sliced (about ½ cup)
2 cups flaked boneless
  smoked whitefish or
  salmon (about ⅔ pound)

Cook rotini as directed on package; drain. Rinse pasta in cold water; drain. Mix mayonnaise, yogurt, dill weed, mustard, salt and pepper in large bowl. Add rotini and remaining ingredients except smoked fish; toss. Gently stir in smoked fish.

RASPBERRY-CHOCOLATE SAUCE

1 package (6 ounces) semi-
  sweet chocolate chips
  (1 cup)
¼ cup sugar
2 tablespoons water
¼ cup half-and-half or milk
1 tablespoon raspberry-
  flavored liqueur

Heat chocolate chips, sugar and water in 1-quart sauce-pan over low heat, stirring constantly, until chips and sugar are melted; remove from heat. Stir in half-and-half and liqueur. Serve warm or cool.

◆ MENU 42 ◆

COD-NEW POTATO SOUP* ◆ HERBED TOMATOES* ◆ CRUSTY FRENCH BREAD

MENU MAKES 4 SERVINGS

INGREDIENTS

1 tablespoon olive or vegetable oil

¼ cup chopped fennel bulb

1 tablespoon chopped fresh or 1 teaspoon dried basil

½ teaspoon salt

¼ teaspoon pepper

Freshly cracked pepper

12 small new potatoes (about 1½ pounds)

8 Italian pear-shaped tomatoes (about ¾ pound)

1 small onion

1 stalk celery

1 pound cod or other lean fish

2 cups half-and-half or milk

½ loaf French bread

1 cup frozen peas

MENU TIP: Cutting all of the vegetable ingredients before cutting the cod for the soup means you won't have to stop and wash the cutting board during meal preparation. By not peeling the tomatoes you'll also save time—and nutrients as well.

TIMETABLE

1. Heat water, salt, pepper and onion to boiling for Cod–New Potato Soup.

2. Cut potatoes into fourths; add to soup.

3. Slice and chop celery for soup and tomatoes, fennel and basil for Herbed Tomatoes.

4. Cut up fish for soup.

5. Add celery, fish and peas to soup.

6. Prepare tomatoes.

7. Add half-and-half to soup.

NUTRITION INFORMATION PER SERVING

Calories	705	**Percent of U.S. RDA**	
Protein, grams	47	Protein	72
Carbohydrate, grams	72	Vitamin A	34
Fat, grams	25	Vitamin C	44
Cholesterol, milligrams	100	Thiamin	26
Sodium, milligrams	1360	Riboflavin	30
Potassium, milligrams	1610	Niacin	38
		Calcium	28
		Iron	74

COD-NEW POTATO SOUP

2 cups water
½ teaspoon salt
¼ teaspoon pepper
1 small onion, chopped
    (about ¼ cup)
12 small new potatoes
    (about 1½ pounds), cut
    into fourths
1 stalk celery (with leaves),
    sliced (about ½ cup)
1 pound cod or other lean
    fish, cut into 1-inch pieces
1 cup frozen peas
2 cups half-and-half or milk

Heat water, salt, pepper and onion to boiling in Dutch oven. Add potatoes. Heat to boiling; reduce heat. Cover and simmer about 10 minutes or until potatoes are almost done.

Add celery, fish and peas. Heat to boiling; reduce heat. Cover and simmer 6 to 8 minutes, stirring gently after 4 minutes, until fish flakes easily with fork. Stir in half-and-half. Heat until hot.

HERBED TOMATOES

8 Italian pear-shaped toma-
    toes (about ¾ pound)
¼ cup chopped fennel bulb
1 tablespoon chopped fresh
    or 1 teaspoon dried basil
1 tablespoon olive or vege-
    table oil
Salt, if desired
Freshly cracked pepper

Slice tomatoes crosswise into ¼-inch slices. Place in 1-quart serving bowl. Sprinkle with fennel and basil. Drizzle with oil. Season to taste with salt and pepper.

GRILLED SHRIMP AND SCALLOP KABOBS* ◆ GRILLED ONIONS* ◆ SAVORY RICE* ◆ WATERMELON WEDGES

MENU MAKES 4 SERVINGS

INGREDIENTS

¼ cup vegetable oil

1 cup uncooked regular long grain rice

2 teaspoons chicken bouillon granules

1 tablespoon toasted pine nuts, if desired

¼ cup lemon juice

2 tablespoons chopped fresh parsley

1 tablespoon chopped fresh or 1 teaspoon dried thyme

¼ teaspoon salt

¼ teaspoon pepper

8 medium whole mushrooms (about 6 ounces)

8 cherry tomatoes

4 medium yellow onions

1 medium zucchini (about 1 inch in diameter)

½ medium watermelon

¾ pound sea scallops

12 raw large shrimp (in shells)

MENU TIP: Since the Grilled Onions and Savory Rice need little attention while cooking, you can still prepare a more involved dish, such as the kabobs, and have everything ready in half-hour.

TIMETABLE

1. If using charcoal grill, start coals before meal preparation.

2. Prepare Grilled Onions.

3. Prepare Savory Rice.

4. Prepare Grilled Shrimp and Scallop Kabobs.

NUTRITION INFORMATION PER SERVING

			Percent of U.S. RDA	
Calories		755		
Protein, grams		40	Protein	60
Carbohydrate, grams		133	Vitamin A	90
Fat, grams		11	Vitamin C	100
Cholesterol, milligrams		115	Thiamin	82
Sodium, milligrams		580	Riboflavin	30
Potassium, milligrams		2190	Niacin	32
			Calcium	10
			Iron	36

GRILLED SHRIMP AND SCALLOP KABOBS

¼ cup lemon juice
¼ cup vegetable oil
1 tablespoon chopped fresh
   or 1 teaspoon dried thyme
¼ teaspoon salt
¼ teaspoon pepper
¾ pound sea scallops
12 raw large shrimp (in
   shells)
8 medium whole mushrooms
   (about 6 ounces)
8 cherry tomatoes
1 medium zucchini (about
   1 inch in diameter), cut
   into 1-inch slices

Mix lemon juice, oil, thyme, salt and pepper. Cut scallops in half if over 1 inch in diameter. Arrange scallops, shrimp and vegetables alternately on four 10-inch metal skewers. Brush with lemon-thyme mixture. Grill 4 inches from medium coals 10 to 15 minutes, brushing with mixture frequently, until scallops are opaque in center and shrimp are pink.

GRILLED ONIONS

4 medium yellow onions

Grill onions 4 inches from medium coals 25 to 30 minutes, turning occasionally, until tender. Carefully remove skins from onions.

SAVORY RICE

1 cup uncooked regular long
   grain rice
2 cups water
2 teaspoons chicken bouillon granules
2 tablespoons chopped fresh
   parsley
1 tablespoon toasted pine
   nuts, if desired

Heat rice, water and bouillon granules to boiling in 2-quart saucepan, stirring once or twice; reduce heat. Cover and simmer 14 minutes. (Do not lift cover or stir.) Remove from heat. Lightly stir in parsley and pine nuts with fork. Cover and let steam 5 to 10 minutes.

MENU
44

Shrimp Fajitas* • Refried Beans with Shredded Cheese • Mexican-style Corn • Mexican Sundaes*

MENU MAKES 4 SERVINGS

INGREDIENTS

1 tablespoon sugar

1 tablespoon cocoa

1 tablespoon vegetable oil

1 teaspoon cornstarch

2 tablespoons instant cinnamon-flavored international coffee mix

1 can (16 ounces) refried beans

1 can (5 ounces) evaporated milk

2 cups Mexican-style corn

1 cup salsa

1 tablespoon lime juice

1½ teaspoons chopped fresh or ½ teaspoon dried oregano

¼ teaspoon ground cumin

1 clove garlic

1 pound raw medium peeled and deveined shrimp

¼ cup shredded cheese (1 ounce)

1 cup guacamole

8 flour tortillas (7 or 8 inches in diameter)

1 pint coffee ice cream

MENU TIP: The tortillas can easily be heated in a microwave instead of the oven. Wrap the tortillas in damp, microwavable paper towels and microwave on high 15 to 20 seconds or until warm. Buying shrimp that are already peeled and cleaned also saves valuable time.

TIMETABLE

1. Heat tortillas for Shrimp Fajitas if using conventional oven.

2. Prepare chocolate sauce for Mexican Sundaes.

3. Prepare beans and corn.

4. Cook shrimp for fajitas.

5. Heat tortillas if using microwave oven.

6. Assemble fajitas.

7. Assemble sundaes after meal.

NUTRITION INFORMATION PER SERVING

Calories	925	**Percent of U.S. RDA**	
Protein, grams	45	Protein	70
Carbohydrates, grams	106	Vitamin A	44
Fat, grams	28	Vitamin C	22
Cholesterol, milligrams	225	Thiamin	22
Sodium, milligrams	2240	Riboflavin	38
Potassium, milligrams	1630	Niacin	24
		Calcium	42
		Iron	68

Shrimp Fajitas

8 flour tortillas (7 or 8
    inches in diameter)
1 tablespoon vegetable oil
1 pound raw medium peeled
    and deveined shrimp
1 tablespoon lime juice
1½ teaspoons chopped fresh
    or ½ teaspoon dried
    oregano
¼ teaspoon ground cumin
1 clove garlic, finely
    chopped
1 cup salsa
1 cup guacamole

Heat oven to 250°. Wrap tortillas in aluminum foil or place on heatproof serving plate and cover with aluminum foil. Heat in oven for about 15 minutes or until warm.

Heat oil in 10-inch skillet over medium heat. Add shrimp, lime juice, oregano, cumin and garlic. Cook about 5 minutes, stirring constantly, until shrimp are pink.

Divide shrimp evenly among tortillas. Top with salsa and guacamole. Fold one end of tortilla up about 1 inch over shrimp mixture. Fold right and left sides over folded end, overlapping. Fold down remaining end. Serve with extra salsa and guacamole if desired.

Mexican Sundaes

1 tablespoon sugar
2 tablespoons instant
    cinnamon-flavored inter-
    national coffee mix
1 tablespoon cocoa
1 teaspoon cornstarch
1 can (5 ounces) evaporated
    milk
1 pint coffee ice cream

Mix sugar, coffee mix, cocoa and cornstarch in 1-quart saucepan. Gradually stir in milk. Heat over medium heat, stirring constantly, until mixture thickens and boils. Boil and stir 1 minute; remove from heat. Cool slightly. Press plastic wrap or waxed paper onto surface. Let stand about 30 minutes.

Spoon ice cream into dessert dishes. Top with warm sauce.

SEAFOOD-PESTO SALAD* • HARD ROLLS WITH GARLIC BUTTER*

MENU MAKES 4 SERVINGS

MENU TIP: Rinsing the cooked pasta in cold water lets you make a pasta salad without extra chilling time. Either commercially prepared or homemade pesto is delightful in this salad.

INGREDIENTS

2 cups uncooked medium shell macaroni (about 5 ounces)

⅓ cup small pitted ripe olives

⅔ cup pesto

2 tablespoons white wine vinegar

1 teaspoon chopped fresh or ½ teaspoon dried oregano

¼ teaspoon paprika

1 clove garlic

Freshly ground pepper

4 ounces spinach

3 Italian pear-shaped tomatoes

1½ cups cooked seafood

2 tablespoons margarine or butter

4 hard rolls

TIMETABLE

1. Heat water to boiling for pasta in Seafood-Pesto Salad.

2. Prepare Garlic Butter. Cover and refrigerate.

3. Cook pasta and prepare seafood salad.

NUTRITION INFORMATION PER SERVING

Calories	690	**Percent of U.S. RDA**	
Protein, grams	25	Protein	38
Carbohydrate, grams	69	Vitamin A	72
Fat, grams	36	Vitamin C	20
Cholesterol, milligrams	45	Thiamin	44
Sodium, milligrams	870	Riboflavin	24
Potassium, milligrams	780	Niacin	28
		Calcium	38
		Iron	42

SEAFOOD–PESTO SALAD

2 cups uncooked medium
  shell macaroni (about
  5 ounces)
⅔ cup pesto
3 Italian pear-shaped tomatoes, cut into eighths
⅓ cup small pitted ripe
  olives
2 tablespoons white wine
  vinegar
4 ounces spinach, coarsely
  chopped (about 3 cups)
1½ cups bite-size pieces
  cooked seafood (scallops,
  lobster, shrimp, crab)

Cook macaroni as directed on package; drain. Rinse in cold water; drain. Mix macaroni, pesto, tomatoes, olives and vinegar in large bowl. Add spinach and seafood. Toss.

GARLIC BUTTER

1 clove garlic, finely
  chopped
2 tablespoons margarine or
  butter, softened
1 teaspoon chopped fresh
  or ½ teaspoon dried
  oregano
¼ teaspoon paprika
Dash of freshly ground
  pepper

Mix all ingredients.

◆ **MENU 46** ◆

TARRAGON-SEAFOOD SALAD* ◆ WHOLE WHEAT CRACKERS AND CREAM CHEESE ◆ CRANBERRY-RASPBERRY TEA* ◆ PEACHY MACAROONS*

MENU MAKES 4 SERVINGS

INGREDIENTS

2 tablespoons olive or vegetable oil

3 cups uncooked bow-shaped macaroni (about 6 ounces)

2 cups iced tea

2 cups cranberry-raspberry juice

2 tablespoons peach brandy

1 dozen whole wheat crackers

1 tablespoon chopped fresh or 1 teaspoon dried tarragon

½ teaspoon salt

¼ teaspoon white pepper

¼ teaspoon ground ginger

2 cloves garlic

4 ounces pea pods

¾ pound seafood sticks

1 cup peach yogurt

¼ cup whipped cream cheese

4 large bakery macaroons

MENU TIP: Cooking the pea pods with the pasta eliminates the need to use a second pot. Use two cups cold water and 2 teaspoons instant tea to make the iced tea for Cranberry-Raspberry Tea.

TIMETABLE

1. Prepare macaroons in Peachy Macaroons and sprinkle with brandy.

2. Prepare Tarragon-Seafood Salad.

3. Prepare Cranberry-Raspberry Tea.

4. Assemble macaroons.

NUTRITION INFORMATION PER SERVING

Calories	600	**Percent of U.S. RDA**	
Protein, grams	21	Protein	32
Carbohydrate, grams	88	Vitamin A	4
Fat, grams	16	Vitamin C	66
Cholesterol, milligrams	25	Thiamin	44
Sodium, milligrams	1190	Riboflavin	28
Potassium, milligrams	700	Niacin	24
		Calcium	12
		Iron	18

TARRAGON-SEAFOOD SALAD

3 cups uncooked bow-shaped macaroni (about 6 ounces)
4 ounces pea pods, cut into halves
2 tablespoons olive or vegetable oil
1 tablespoon chopped fresh or 1 teaspoon dried tarragon
½ teaspoon salt
¼ teaspoon white pepper
2 cloves garlic, finely chopped
¾ pound seafood sticks, cut into ½-inch pieces

Cook macaroni as directed on package—except add pea pods 1 minute before pasta is done; drain. Rinse pasta and pea pods in cold water; drain. Gently toss all ingredients.

CRANBERRY-RASPBERRY TEA

2 cups iced tea
2 cups cranberry-raspberry juice

Mix tea and juice. Serve over ice.

PEACHY MACAROONS

4 large bakery macaroons
2 tablespoons peach brandy
¼ teaspoon ground ginger
1 cup peach yogurt

Cut each macaroon into fourths to within ¼ inch of bottom. Gently spread open. Place macaroons in individual dessert dishes. Sprinkle brandy over macaroons. Let stand 30 minutes. Stir ginger into yogurt. Spoon yogurt over macaroons.

Quick Jambalaya* • Breadsticks • Honey Ambrosia*

MENU MAKES 4 SERVINGS

INGREDIENTS

1 tablespoon honey

2 tablespoons flaked coconut

1 tablespoon lemon juice

1½ cups uncooked instant rice

1 can (14½ ounces) stewed tomatoes, undrained

⅛ teaspoon ground red pepper (cayenne)

1 teaspoon chopped fresh or ¼ teaspoon dried thyme

2 teaspoons chicken bouillon granules

¼ teaspoon chili powder

1 small onion

½ medium green bell pepper

3 medium oranges

1 medium banana

¼ cup orange juice

1 package (10 ounces) frozen quick-cooking shrimp

1 package (8 ounces) brown-and-serve sausage links

8 dry breadsticks

MENU TIP: Brown-and-serve sausages and quick-cooking shrimp bring the flavor of authenticity to Quick Jambalaya, a traditionally long-cooking dish.

TIMETABLE

1. Prepare Quick Jambalaya.
2. Prepare Honey Ambrosia.

NUTRITION INFORMATION PER SERVING

		Percent of U.S. RDA	
Calories	680		
Protein, grams	31	Protein	46
Carbohydrate, grams	120	Vitamin A	20
Fat, grams	10	Vitamin C	88
Cholesterol, milligrams	125	Thiamin	42
Sodium, milligrams	1060	Riboflavin	10
Potassium, milligrams	860	Niacin	28
		Calcium	8
		Iron	36

QUICK JAMBALAYA

1 package (8 ounces) brown-and-serve sausage links
1½ cups uncooked instant rice
1½ cups water
1 can (14½ ounces) stewed tomatoes, undrained
1 package (10 ounces) frozen quick-cooking shrimp
1 small onion, chopped (about ¼ cup)
½ medium green bell pepper, chopped
2 teaspoons chicken bouillon granules
1 teaspoon chopped fresh or ¼ teaspoon dried thyme
¼ teaspoon chili powder
⅛ teaspoon ground red pepper (cayenne)

Cut sausages into 1-inch diagonal slices. Cook in 10-inch skillet according to package directions; drain. Add remaining ingredients to skillet. Heat boiling, stirring occasionally; reduce heat. Simmer uncovered 10 minutes, stirring occasionally.

HONEY AMBROSIA

¼ cup orange juice
1 tablespoon honey
1 tablespoon lemon juice
3 medium oranges, pared and thinly sliced
1 medium banana, sliced
2 tablespoons flaked coconut

Mix orange juice, honey and lemon juice in medium bowl. Gently stir in oranges, banana and coconut.

◆ MENU
48

AVOCADO-CRAB SOUP* ◆ CHEDDAR-CORN MUFFINS* ◆ TOSSED SALAD WITH FRENCH DRESSING

MENU MAKES 4 SERVINGS

INGREDIENTS

1 cup all-purpose flour

1 cup yellow cornmeal

2 tablespoons sugar

¼ cup vegetable oil

4 teaspoons baking powder

1 can (10¾ ounces) condensed chicken broth

¼ cup French dressing

1 tablespoon lemon juice

½ teaspoon salt

1 small clove garlic

2 cups salad greens

1 medium tomato

2 medium avocados

1 green onion

1 cup milk

1 cup plain yogurt

½ cup shredded Cheddar cheese (2 ounces)

1 egg

1 package (6 ounces) frozen crabmeat

MENU TIP: The Cheddar-Corn Muffins call for paper baking cups instead of greasing the pan; it's faster and saves on calories! Nutrition information has been calculated for 1 muffin per serving.

TIMETABLE

1. Prepare Cheddar-Corn Muffins.

2. Cut green onions and avocados for Avocado-Crab Soup.

3. Prepare salad ingredients.

4. Prepare soup.

5. Toss salad.

NUTRITION INFORMATION PER SERVING

Calories	505	**Percent of U.S. RDA**	
Protein, grams	17	Protein	26
Carbohydrate, grams	38	Vitamin A	20
Fat, grams	33	Vitamin C	8
Cholesterol, milligrams	50	Thiamin	20
Sodium, milligrams	1350	Riboflavin	24
Potassium, milligrams	930	Niacin	22
		Calcium	24
		Iron	14

AVOCADO-CRAB SOUP

1 can (10¾ ounces) con-
  densed chicken broth
1 cup water
1 green onion (with top),
  cut into about 1-inch
  pieces
1 small clove garlic
1 tablespoon lemon juice
2 medium avocados, pared
  and cut up
1 cup plain yogurt
1 package (6 ounces) fro-
  zen crabmeat, thawed

Heat chicken broth, water, green onion and garlic to boiling in 2-quart saucepan. Pour hot mixture into food processor or blender. Add lemon juice and avocados. Cover and process or blend about 30 seconds or until smooth.

Pour mixture back into saucepan. Stir in yogurt and crabmeat. Heat, stirring constantly, just until hot.

*1 can (6 ounces) crabmeat, drained, or 1 package (8 ounces) salad-style imitation crabmeat can be substituted for the frozen crabmeat.

CHEDDAR-CORN MUFFINS

1 cup yellow cornmeal
1 cup all-purpose flour
2 tablespoons sugar
4 teaspoons baking powder
½ teaspoon salt
1 cup milk
½ cup shredded Cheddar
  cheese (2 ounces)
¼ cup vegetable oil
1 egg

Heat oven to 425°. Line 12 medium muffin cups, 2½ × 1¼ inches, with paper baking cups. Mix all ingredients. Beat vigorously 1 minute. Divide batter evenly among muffin cups. Bake about 15 minutes or until golden brown. **12 muffins, 1 per serving.**

#58 (page 164)

CHAPTER 5

MEATLESS

HOME-STYLE SCRAMBLED EGGS* • SESAME FINGERS* • CANTALOUPE WEDGES

MENU MAKES 4 SERVINGS

INGREDIENTS

2 teaspoons sesame seed

½ teaspoon salt

3 tablespoons finely chopped onion

1 medium potato, cooked

1 medium tomato

1 small zucchini

1 medium cantaloupe

¼ cup (½ stick) margarine or butter

4 eggs

4 slices whole wheat bread

MENU TIP: Home-style Scrambled Eggs is a great dish to make with a leftover baked potato, or microwave a potato immediately before starting the recipe. Pierce potato with knife to allow steam to escape and place on microwavable paper towel. Microwave on high for 5 to 6 minutes; let stand 5 minutes.

TIMETABLE

1. Microwave potato for Home-style Scrambled Eggs if necessary (see Menu Tip).

2. Prepare Sesame Fingers for broiling.

3. Cut cantaloupe into wedges.

4. Prepare Home-style Scrambled Eggs.

5. Broil Sesame Fingers.

NUTRITION INFORMATION PER SERVING

		Percent of U.S. RDA	
Calories	365		
Protein, grams	13	Protein	20
Carbohydrate, grams	42	Vitamin A	100
Fat, grams	18	Vitamin C	100
Cholesterol, milligrams	215	Thiamin	16
Sodium, milligrams	640	Riboflavin	24
Potassium, milligrams	1070	Niacin	14
		Calcium	12
		Iron	30

HOME-STYLE SCRAMBLED EGGS

4 eggs
3 tablespoons water
½ teaspoon salt
2 tablespoons margarine or
    butter
3 tablespoons finely chopped
    onion
1 medium potato, cooked
    and cubed (about 1 cup)
1 medium tomato, seeded
    and chopped
1 small zucchini, chopped

Beat eggs, water and salt with fork; set aside. Heat margarine in 10-inch skillet over medium heat until melted. Cook and stir vegetables in margarine 2 minutes. Pour egg mixture into skillet.

As mixture begins to set at bottom and side, gently lift cooked portions with spatula so that thin, uncooked portion can flow to bottom. Avoid constant stirring. Cook 3 to 5 minutes or until eggs are thickened throughout but still moist.

SESAME FINGERS

4 slices whole wheat bread
2 tablespoons margarine or
    butter, softened
2 teaspoons sesame seed

Set oven control to broil. Spread bread with margarine. Sprinkle with sesame seed. Cut each slice crosswise into 4 strips. Place strips in broiler pan. Broil 4 inches from heat 1½ to 2 minutes or until edges of bread are brown.

MENU
50

SAVORY EGG POCKETS* • CREAMY HONEY SALAD*

MENU MAKES 4 SERVINGS

INGREDIENTS

2 tablespoons honey

¼ cup honey-roasted peanuts

1 teaspoon Worcestershire sauce

1 tablespoon chopped fresh parsley or 1 teaspoon parsley flakes

¼ teaspoon dry mustard

¼ teaspoon salt

½ cup alfalfa sprouts

¼ cup chopped green bell pepper

2 medium stalks celery

1 small tomato

2 tart red apples

⅓ cup plain yogurt

¼ cup shredded Cheddar cheese (1 ounce)

2 tablespoons margarine or butter

8 eggs

2 pita breads (6 inches in diameter)

MENU TIP: Mixing the Creamy Honey Dressing in the bowl before adding the salad ingredients means you won't have to use a separate bowl just for the dressing.

TIMETABLE

1. Prepare Creamy Honey Dressing.

2. Chop tomato and bell pepper for Savory Egg Pockets.

3. Cut apples and celery for Creamy Honey Salad.

4. Finish salad.

5. Prepare Savory Egg Pockets.

NUTRITION INFORMATION PER SERVING

		Percent of U.S. RDA	
Calories	485		
Protein, grams	21	Protein	32
Carbohydrate, grams	47	Vitamin A	26
Fat, grams	23	Vitamin C	20
Cholesterol, milligrams	435	Thiamin	8
Sodium, milligrams	410	Riboflavin	36
Potassium, milligrams	430	Niacin	10
		Calcium	14
		Iron	12

SAVORY EGG POCKETS

2 tablespoons margarine or
butter
¼ cup chopped green bell
pepper
1 small tomato, seeded and
chopped (about ½ cup)
8 eggs
1 teaspoon Worcestershire
sauce
¼ teaspoon salt
2 pita breads (6 inches in
diameter), cut in half
and opened to form pockets
½ cup alfalfa sprouts

Heat margarine in 10-inch skillet over medium heat until melted. Cook bell pepper and tomato in margarine about 3 minutes, stirring occasionally, until bell pepper is tender. Mix eggs, Worcestershire sauce and salt. Pour into skillet.

As mixture begins to set at bottom and side, gently lift cooked portions with spatula so that thin, uncooked portion can flow to bottom. Avoid constant stirring. Cook 3 to 5 minutes or until eggs are thickened throughout but still moist. Spoon into pita breads. Top with alfalfa sprouts.

CREAMY HONEY SALAD

Creamy Honey Dressing
(below)
2 unpared tart red apples,
cut into cubes
2 medium stalks celery, sliced
¼ cup honey-roasted peanuts
¼ cup shredded Cheddar
cheese (1 ounce)

Prepare Creamy Honey Dressing in medium bowl. Stir in remaining ingredients.

Creamy Honey Dressing

⅓ cup plain yogurt
1 tablespoon chopped fresh
parsley or 1 teaspoon
parsley flakes
2 tablespoons honey
¼ teaspoon dry mustard

Mix all ingredients.

Menu #50 (page 143)

COUSCOUS* ◆ GARBANZO BEANS AND VEGETABLES* ◆ EASY SWEET YOGURT*

MENU MAKES 4 SERVINGS

INGREDIENTS

1 tablespoon olive or vegetable oil

¾ cup uncooked quick-cooking couscous

⅓ cup raisins

1 can (15 ounces) garbanzo beans (chick-peas)

1 teaspoon chicken bouillon granules

1 teaspoon ground coriander

¾ teaspoon salt

½ teaspoon ground cardamom

¼ teaspoon ground turmeric

⅛ teaspoon ground nutmeg

⅛ teaspoon ground red pepper (cayenne)

2 cloves garlic

2 cups sliced carrots

2 medium zucchini

1 medium onion

1 container (18 ounces) vanilla yogurt

2 tablespoons margarine or butter

MENU TIP: Couscous is a granular pasta made from pre-cooked semolina that rehydrates in only a few minutes. Purchase sliced carrots either from a salad bar or frozen. Rinse frozen carrots under running water to thaw and then drain.

TIMETABLE

1. Prepare Garbanzo Beans and Vegetables.

2. Prepare and refrigerate Easy Sweet Yogurt.

3. Prepare Couscous.

4. Spoon yogurt into dessert dishes.

NUTRITION INFORMATION PER SERVING

Calories	505	**Percent of U.S. RDA**	
Protein, grams	16	Protein	24
Carbohydrate, grams	78	Vitamin A	100
Fat, grams	15	Vitamin C	12
Cholesterol, milligrams	15	Thiamin	14
Sodium, milligrams	1000	Riboflavin	18
Potassium, milligrams	910	Niacin	10
		Calcium	24
		Iron	16

Couscous

1¼ cups water
⅓ cup raisins
2 tablespoons margarine or butter
¼ teaspoon salt
¾ cup uncooked quick-cooking couscous

Heat water, raisins, margarine and salt to boiling in 1-quart saucepan. Stir in couscous; cover. Remove from heat and let stand covered 5 minutes.

Garbanzo Beans and Vegetables

1 tablespoon olive or vegetable oil
1 medium onion, sliced
2 cloves garlic, finely chopped
2 cups sliced carrots
2 medium zucchini, sliced
1 can (15 ounces) garbanzo beans, undrained
1 teaspoon ground coriander
1 teaspoon chicken bouillon granules
½ teaspoon salt
¼ teaspoon ground turmeric
⅛ teaspoon ground red pepper (cayenne)

Heat oil in 3-quart saucepan over medium-high heat. Sauté onion and garlic 3 minutes. Stir in remaining ingredients. Heat to boiling; reduce heat. Cover and simmer 12 to 15 minutes or until vegetables are crisp-tender. Serve over Couscous.

Easy Sweet Yogurt

1 container (18 ounces) vanilla yogurt
½ teaspoon ground cardamom
⅛ teaspoon ground nutmeg

Mix all ingredients. Cover and refrigerate until serving time.

SAVORY BLACK-EYED PEAS* • TOASTED BAGEL ROUNDS* • ANGEL FOOD CAKE WITH STRAWBERRY-KIWI SAUCE*

MENU MAKES 4 SERVINGS

INGREDIENTS

½ cup uncooked regular long grain rice

1 tablespoon orange-flavored liqueur

1 can (16 ounces) black-eyed peas

1 can (16 ounces) stewed tomatoes

¼ teaspoon salt

¼ teaspoon garlic powder

¼ teaspoon ground cinnamon

⅛ teaspoon pepper

Dash of ground red pepper (cayenne)

¼ cup chopped green bell pepper

2 tablespoons chopped fresh parsley

1 small zucchini

1 kiwifruit

¼ cup (½ stick) margarine or butter

4 slices angel food cake

2 plain bagels

1 package (10 ounces) frozen strawberries in syrup

MENU TIP: Combining fresh with canned or frozen produce is a quick way to prepare fresh-tasting dishes. We've done just that for the black-eyed peas and the fruit sauce.

TIMETABLE

1. Prepare Savory Black-eyed Peas.

2. Prepare Toasted Bagel Rounds for broiling.

3. Prepare Strawberry-Kiwi Sauce.

4. Broil rounds.

5. After meal place angel food cake on serving plates; top with sauce.

NUTRITION INFORMATION PER SERVING

		Percent of U.S. RDA	
Calories	650		
Protein, grams	16	Protein	24
Carbohydrate, grams	114	Vitamin A	40
Fat, grams	16	Vitamin C	76
Cholesterol, milligrams	5	Thiamin	38
Sodium, milligrams	1110	Riboflavin	18
Potassium, milligrams	860	Niacin	20
		Calcium	12
		Iron	26

SAVORY BLACK-EYED PEAS

½ cup uncooked regular long grain rice
½ cup water
¼ cup chopped green bell pepper
1 small zucchini, sliced
¼ teaspoon salt
⅛ teaspoon pepper
1 can (16 ounces) black-eyed peas, drained
1 can (16 ounces) stewed tomatoes, undrained
2 tablespoons chopped fresh parsley

Heat all ingredients except parsley to boiling in 2-quart saucepan; reduce heat. Cover and simmer 20 minutes. Stir in parsley.

TOASTED BAGEL ROUNDS

2 plain bagels
3 tablespoons margarine or butter, softened
¼ teaspoon garlic powder
Dash of ground red pepper (cayenne)

Set oven control to broil. Cut each bagel horizontally into 4 rounds. Mix margarine, garlic powder and red pepper. Spread over bagel rounds. Place bagel rounds on ungreased cookie sheet. Broil 6 inches from heat 1½ to 2 minutes or until light brown.

STRAWBERRY-KIWI SAUCE

1 package (10 ounces) frozen strawberries in syrup
1 tablespoon margarine or butter
1 tablespoon orange-flavored liqueur
¼ teaspoon ground cinnamon
1 kiwifruit, pared and chopped

Heat strawberries in 1½-quart saucepan over medium-low heat, stirring occasionally, until thawed. Stir in remaining ingredients. Cook and stir 1 minute or until margarine is melted. Serve over angel food cake.

MENU
53

Refried-Bean Roll-ups* • Carrots with Grapes* • Banana Cream*

MENU MAKES 4 SERVINGS

INGREDIENTS

2 tablespoons powdered sugar

1½ teaspoons granulated sugar

½ cup salsa

1 can (16 ounces) refried beans

½ teaspoon lemon juice

1 teaspoon chopped fresh or ¼ teaspoon dried tarragon

½ teaspoon chili powder

¼ teaspoon salt

⅛ teaspoon ground cinnamon

1 cup shredded lettuce

1½ cups seedless green grapes

2 medium ripe bananas

½ cup shredded Monterey Jack cheese (2 ounces)

⅓ cup sour cream

¼ cup whipping (heavy) cream

1 tablespoon margarine or butter

8 flour tortillas (7 to 8 inches in diameter)

1½ cups frozen sliced carrots

MENU TIP: The tortillas for the Refried-Bean Roll-ups can easily be warmed in a microwave instead of the oven. Wrap the tortillas in damp microwavable paper towels and microwave on high 15 to 20 seconds or until warm.

TIMETABLE

1. Heat tortillas for Refried-Bean Roll-ups if using conventional oven.

2. Cook carrots for Carrots with Grapes.

3. Prepare bean mixture for roll-ups.

4. Add remaining ingredients to carrots.

5. Warm tortillas if using microwave oven (see Menu Tip).

6. Assemble roll-ups.

7. Prepare Banana Cream.

NUTRITION INFORMATION PER SERVING

Calories	535	**Percent of U.S. RDA**	
Protein, grams	16	Protein	24
Carbohydrate, grams	79	Vitamin A	50
Fat, grams	20	Vitamin C	26
Cholesterol, milligrams	45	Thiamin	16
Sodium, milligrams	1100	Riboflavin	18
Potassium, milligrams	1070	Niacin	10
		Calcium	30
		Iron	28

REFRIED-BEAN ROLL-UPS

8 flour tortillas (7 to 8 inches
    in diameter)
1 can (16 ounces) refried
    beans
½ cup salsa
½ teaspoon chili powder
1 cup shredded lettuce
½ cup shredded Monterey
    Jack cheese (2 ounces)

Heat oven to 250°. Wrap tortillas in aluminum foil or place on heatproof serving plate and cover with aluminum foil. Heat about 15 minutes or until warm.

Mix beans, salsa and chili powder in saucepan. Heat over medium heat 5 minutes, stirring occasionally, until warm. Place about ¼ cup mixture in center of each tortilla; spread slightly. Top with about 2 tablespoons lettuce and 1 tablespoon cheese. Fold over sides and ends. Serve with extra salsa if desired.

CARROTS WITH GRAPES

1½ cups frozen sliced carrots
1½ cups seedless green
    grapes
1 tablespoon margarine or
    butter
1½ teaspoons granulated
    sugar
1 teaspoon chopped fresh or
    ¼ teaspoon dried
    tarragon
¼ teaspoon salt
⅓ cup sour cream
1 tablespoon water

Cook carrots as directed on package; drain. Stir in grapes, margarine, sugar, tarragon and salt. Cook 3 minutes, stirring occasionally; remove from heat. Stir in sour cream and water.

BANANA CREAM

2 medium ripe bananas, cut
    into fourths
¼ cup whipping (heavy)
    cream
2 tablespoons powdered sugar
⅛ teaspoon ground cinnamon
½ teaspoon lemon juice

Place all ingredients in blender. Cover and blend until smooth.

◆ MENU 54 ◆

BLACK BEAN SALAD* ◆ CHILI-CHEESE TORTILLAS*

MENU MAKES 4 SERVINGS

INGREDIENTS

2 tablespoons vegetable oil

2 cans (15 ounces each) black beans

1 can (4 ounces) diced green chilies

¼ cup red wine vinegar

½ teaspoon chili powder

¼ teaspoon ground cumin

1 small clove garlic

1 cup diced jicama (about 5 ounces)

2 green onions

1 medium tomato

1 cup shredded Cheddar cheese (4 ounces)

8 flour tortillas (7 to 8 inches in diameter)

1 cup frozen whole kernel corn

MENU TIP: Canned black beans easily incorporate this nutritious and delicious legume into your diet. The Chili-Cheese Tortillas can be microwaved on high 2 to 3 minutes; cover a microwavable dish with a damp microwavable paper towel instead of aluminum foil. Buying prediced chilies cuts down on chopping time.

TIMETABLE

1. Heat oven.

2. Prepare Chili Dressing for Black Bean Salad.

3. Prepare Chili-Cheese Tortillas if using conventional oven.

4. Prepare Black Bean Salad.

5. Prepare Chili-Cheese Tortillas if using microwave oven (see Menu Tip).

NUTRITION INFORMATION PER SERVING

		Percent of U.S. RDA	
Calories	530		
Protein, grams	24	Protein	36
Carbohydrate, grams	71	Vitamin A	24
Fat, grams	19	Vitamin C	22
Cholesterol, milligrams	30	Thiamin	30
Sodium, milligrams	270	Riboflavin	14
Potassium, milligrams	810	Niacin	8
		Calcium	36
		Iron	30

BLACK BEAN SALAD

Chili Dressing (below)
1 cup frozen whole kernel corn, rinsed to thaw and drained
1 cup diced jicama (about 5 ounces)
1 medium tomato, seeded and chopped (about ¾ cup)
2 cans (15 ounces each) black beans, rinsed and drained
2 green onions (with tops), sliced

Prepare Chili Dressing in large glass or plastic bowl. Stir in remaining ingredients.

¼ cup red wine vinegar
2 tablespoons vegetable oil
½ teaspoon chili powder
¼ teaspoon ground cumin
1 small clove garlic, crushed

Chili Dressing
Mix all ingredients.

CHILI-CHEESE TORTILLAS

1 can (4 ounces) diced green chilies, drained
8 flour tortillas (7 to 8 inches in diameter)
1 cup shredded Cheddar cheese (4 ounces)

Heat oven to 350°. Spread about 1 tablespoon chilies on each tortilla. Sprinkle each with scant 2 tablespoons cheese. Roll up tightly. (Secure with toothpicks if necessary.) Place with seam sides down in ungreased square pan, 9 × 9 × 2 inches. Cover with aluminum foil. Bake about 15 minutes or until warm.

MENU
55

MACARONI AND CHEESE WITH GREEN CHILIES* • BROCCOLI SPEARS WITH HUMMUS SAUCE* • RED GRAPES

MENU MAKES 4 SERVINGS

INGREDIENTS

2 cups uncooked shell macaroni (about 8 ounces)

1 cup canned garbanzo beans

¼ cup sliced pitted ripe olives

1 can (4 ounces) chopped green chilies

1 tablespoon lime juice

1 tablespoon packed fresh cilantro or parsley

¾ teaspoon salt

1 pound broccoli spears

½ cup chopped red bell pepper or 1 jar (2 ounces) diced pimientos

Red grapes (1 pound)

½ cup milk

½ cup shredded Cheddar cheese (2 ounces)

½ cup plain yogurt

MENU TIP: Canned sliced olives and shredded Cheddar cheese give you a head start on the macaroni. A 16-ounce can of garbanzo beans has about 1¾ cups beans and the Hummus Sauce needs 1 cup. Use the remaining beans in a salad or soup the next day.

TIMETABLE

1. Cook macaroni for Macaroni and Cheese with Green Chilies.

2. Prepare Hummus Sauce for Broccoli Spears with Hummus Sauce.

3. Steam broccoli.

4. Stir remaining ingredients into macaroni.

NUTRITION INFORMATION PER SERVING

		Percent of U.S. RDA	
Calories	510		
Protein, grams	20	Protein	30
Carbohydrate, grams	88	Vitamin A	42
Fat, grams	10	Vitamin C	100
Cholesterol, milligrams	20	Thiamin	20
Sodium, milligrams	790	Riboflavin	30
Potassium, milligrams	830	Niacin	12
		Calcium	34
		Iron	20

MACARONI AND CHEESE WITH GREEN CHILIES

2 cups uncooked shell macaroni (about 8 ounces)
½ cup milk
½ cup shredded Cheddar cheese (2 ounces)
½ cup chopped red bell pepper or 1 jar (2 ounces) diced pimientos, drained
¼ cup sliced pitted ripe olives
1 can (4 ounces) chopped green chilies, drained
½ teaspoon salt

Cook macaroni as directed on package; drain. Stir in remaining ingredients. Cook over low heat about 5 minutes, stirring occasionally, until cheese is melted and sauce is hot.

BROCCOLI SPEARS WITH HUMMUS SAUCE

Hummus Sauce (below)
1 pound broccoli spears

Prepare Hummus Sauce. Place steamer basket in ½ inch water (water should not touch bottom of basket). Place broccoli in basket. Cover tightly and heat to boiling; reduce heat. Steam about 12 minutes or until stems are tender. Serve sauce over broccoli.

Hummus Sauce

1 cup canned garbanzo beans
½ cup plain yogurt
1 tablespoon packed fresh cilantro or parsley
1 tablespoon lime juice
¼ teaspoon salt

Place all ingredients in food processor or blender. Cover and process or blend until smooth.

◇ MENU
56

RICE NOODLES WITH PEANUT SAUCE* ◆
CUCUMBER SALAD* ◆ LIME BANANAS*

MENU MAKES 4 SERVINGS

INGREDIENTS

½ cup creamy peanut butter

2 tablespoons packed brown sugar

1 tablespoon granulated sugar

8 ounces uncooked rice stick noodles

½ cup chicken broth or water

2 tablespoons rice or cider vinegar

2 tablespoons soy sauce

1 teaspoon fish sauce or ⅛ teaspoon salt

2 tablespoons chopped fresh cilantro, if desired

1 teaspoon grated gingerroot

½ teaspoon crushed red pepper

Dash of ground red pepper (cayenne)

1 clove garlic

4 ounces bean sprouts

2 green onions

1 medium cucumber

1 red bell pepper

3 large firm ripe bananas

½ small lime

2 tablespoons margarine

MENU TIP: Using rice stick noodles that cook in only 1 minute makes a quick pasta dish. Fish sauce is available in Asian markets or the ethnic section of many supermarkets. Squeeze the lime juice directly from the lime half onto the bananas and you won't need a juicer.

TIMETABLE

1. Heat water for noodles.

2. Prepare vegetables for Rice Noodles with Peanut Sauce and Cucumber Salad.

3. Prepare salad.

4. Finish noodle dish.

5. Prepare Lime Bananas.

NUTRITION INFORMATION PER SERVING

Calories	595	**Percent of U.S. RDA**	
Protein, grams	20	Protein	30
Carbohydrate, grams	87	Vitamin A	18
Fat, grams	24	Vitamin C	100
Cholesterol, milligrams	0	Thiamin	28
Sodium, milligrams	1380	Riboflavin	16
Potassium, milligrams	1020	Niacin	40
		Calcium	6
		Iron	22

Menu #56 (page 157)

RICE NOODLES WITH PEANUT SAUCE

2 quarts water
½ cup creamy peanut butter
2 tablespoons soy sauce
1 teaspoon grated gingerroot
½ teaspoon crushed red
   pepper
½ cup chicken broth or water
8 ounces uncooked rice stick
   noodles
4 ounces bean sprouts
1 red bell pepper, cut into
   fourths and sliced thinly
   crosswise
2 green onions (with tops),
   sliced
2 tablespoons chopped fresh
   cilantro, if desired.

Heat 2 quarts water to boiling. Mix peanut butter, soy sauce, gingerroot and red pepper until smooth. Gradually stir in chicken broth. Break noodles in half and pull apart slightly while dropping into boiling water. Cook uncovered 1 minute; drain. Rinse in cold water; drain. Place noodles in large bowl. Add peanut butter mixture, bean sprouts, bell pepper and green onions; toss. Sprinkle with cilantro.

CUCUMBER SALAD

1 tablespoon granulated
   sugar
2 tablespoons rice or cider
   vinegar
1 teaspoon fish sauce or
   ⅛ teaspoon salt
Dash of ground red pepper
   (cayenne)
1 clove garlic, finely chopped
1 medium cucumber, pared,
   cut in half lengthwise
   and sliced

Mix all ingredients except cucumber in medium bowl until sugar is dissolved. Stir in cucumber.

LIME BANANAS

3 large firm ripe bananas
2 tablespoons packed brown
   sugar
2 tablespoons margarine
½ small lime, seeded

Cut each banana crosswise in half, then lengthwise in half. Heat brown sugar and margarine in 10-inch skillet over medium-low heat, stirring constantly, until melted and bubbly. Place bananas in single layer in skillet. Cook uncovered 3 to 4 minutes, turning occasionally, until bananas are soft. Squeeze lime over bananas.

MENU
57

TORTELLINI IN BALSAMIC VINAIGRETTE* ◆ APPLE-PINEAPPLE SAUCE* ◆ PARMESAN ENGLISH MUFFINS*

MENU MAKES 4 SERVINGS

INGREDIENTS

2 tablespoons olive or vegetable oil

1 package (7 ounces) uncooked tricolor cheese tortellini

1 can (8 ounces) pineapple tidbits

1 cup applesauce

¼ cup balsamic or cider vinegar

1 tablespoon chopped fresh or 1 teaspoon dried basil

½ teaspoon Italian seasoning

¼ teaspoon paprika

¼ teaspoon ground cinnamon

⅛ teaspoon salt

1 clove garlic

2 cups broccoli flowerets

2 green onions

1 medium carrot

2 tablespoons margarine or butter

2 tablespoons grated Parmesan cheese

2 whole wheat English muffins

MENU TIP: Prepare the Balsamic Vinaigrette and stir in the remaining ingredients while the tortellini is cooking. This gives the vegetables time to marinate and the dish can be quickly completed by stirring in the tortellini when it is cooked.

TIMETABLE

1. Prepare Tortellini in Balsamic Vinaigrette.

2. Prepare Apple-Pineapple Sauce.

3. Prepare Parmesan English Muffins.

NUTRITION INFORMATION PER SERVING

		Percent of U.S. RDA	
Calories	445		
Protein, grams	10	Protein	16
Carbohydrate, grams	70	Vitamin A	100
Fat, grams	14	Vitamin C	26
Cholesterol, milligrams	0	Thiamin	42
Sodium, milligrams	300	Riboflavin	22
Potassium, milligrams	350	Niacin	24
		Calcium	14
		Iron	20

TORTELLINI IN BALSAMIC VINAIGRETTE

1 package (7 ounces) un-cooked tricolor cheese tortellini
Balsamic Vinaigrette (below)
1 medium carrot, sliced
2 cups broccoli flowerets
2 green onions (with tops), sliced

Cook tortellini as directed on package; drain. Rinse with cold water; drain.

Prepare Balsamic Vinaigrette in large bowl. Stir in remaining ingredients except tortellini. Stir in tortellini.

¼ cup balsamic or cider vinegar
2 tablespoons olive or vegetable oil
1 tablespoon chopped fresh or 1 teaspoon dried basil
¼ teaspoon paprika
⅛ teaspoon salt
1 clove garlic, crushed

Balsamic Vinaigrette
Mix all ingredients.

APPLE-PINEAPPLE SAUCE

1 cup applesauce
1 can (8 ounces) pineapple tidbits, drained
¼ teaspoon ground cinnamon

Mix all ingredients.

PARMESAN ENGLISH MUFFINS

2 tablespoons margarine or butter, softened
2 whole wheat English muffins, split
2 tablespoons grated Parmesan cheese
½ teaspoon Italian seasoning

Set oven control to broil. Spread margarine on muffin halves. Sprinkle with Parmesan cheese and Italian seasoning. Cut each muffin half in half. Place in broiler pan. Broil 4 inches from heat about 2 minutes or until light brown.

Menu #57 (page 161)

**MENU
58**

PITA PIZZAS* • FRUIT AND GREENS
SALADS* • ASSORTED COOKIES

MENU MAKES 4 SERVINGS

INGREDIENTS

1 can (15½ ounces) great
  northern beans

1 can (11 ounces) pineapple
  and mandarin orange
  segments

3 tablespoons fruit salad
  dressing

8 assorted cookies

2 tablespoons chopped fresh
  or 2 teaspoons dried basil

¼ teaspoon salt

1 small clove garlic

2 cups bite-size salad greens

2 tablespoons chopped red
  onion

1 large tomato

1 large green bell pepper

1 small onion

1 cup shredded part-skim
  mozzarella cheese
  (4 ounces)

4 whole wheat pita breads
  (4 inches in diameter)

MENU TIP: These two recipes can be made quickly using
cut vegetables from the salad bar. If you cut them
yourself, chop and cut up all vegetables at once; then
prepare recipes. The liquid from the canned beans in
the pizzas can be drained directly into the skillet.

TIMETABLE

1. Chop or cut up all vegetables for both recipes.

2. Prepare Pita Pizzas.

3. Prepare Fruit and Greens Salad.

NUTRITION INFORMATION PER SERVING

Calories	520	**Percent of U.S. RDA**		
Protein, grams	24	Protein	36
Carbohydrate, grams	83	Vitamin A	18
Fat, grams	9	Vitamin C	52
Cholesterol, milligrams	35	Thiamin	14
Sodium, milligrams	710	Riboflavin	12
Potassium, milligrams	650	Niacin	6
		Calcium	30
		Iron	20

PITA PIZZAS

4 whole wheat pita breads
(4 inches in diameter)
1 small onion, chopped
(about ¼ cup)
1 small clove garlic, finely
chopped
1 can (15½ ounces) great
northern beans, drained
and liquid reserved
2 tablespoons chopped fresh
or 2 teaspoons dried basil
¼ teaspoon salt
1 large tomato, seeded and
cut into ¼-inch pieces
1 large green bell pepper,
cut into 16 thin rings
1 cup shredded part-skim
mozzarella cheese
(4 ounces)

Heat oven to 425°. Split each pita bread in half around edge with knife. Place in ungreased jelly roll pan, 15½ × 10½ × 1 inch. Bake uncovered about 5 minutes or just until crisp. Cook onion and garlic in reserved bean liquid in 10-inch nonstick skillet over medium heat about 5 minutes, stirring occasionally. Stir in beans; heat through.

Place bean mixture, basil and salt in blender or food processor. Cover and blend or process until smooth. Spread about 2 tablespoons bean mixture on each pita bread half. Top each with tomato, bell pepper and cheese. Bake 5 to 7 minutes or until cheese is melted.

FRUIT AND GREENS SALAD

2 cups bite-size salad greens
2 tablespoons chopped red
onion
1 can (11 ounces) pineap-
ple and mandarin orange
segments, well drained
3 tablespoons fruit salad
dressing

Mix all ingredients.

Menu #61 (page 174)

CHAPTER 6
MICROWAVE

SHERRIED HAM DIJON* • SWEET POTATOES • SPINACH SALAD*

MENU MAKES 4 SERVINGS

INGREDIENTS

1 teaspoon sugar

1 tablespoon sherry, dry white wine or apple juice

3 tablespoons cider vinegar

2 tablespoons Dijon mustard

2 tablespoons mustard seed

¼ teaspoon dry mustard

Chopped fresh parsley, if desired

¼ teaspoon pepper

Freshly ground pepper

¾ pound spinach

3 ounces mushrooms

1 small onion

1 can (18 ounces) sweet potatoes or yams or 4 fresh sweet potatoes

3 slices bacon

1 fully cooked smoked ham slice, about 1 inch thick (about 1 pound)

2 tablespoons grated Parmesan cheese

1 hard-cooked egg

MENU TIP: Canned sweet potatoes, drained and placed in a microwavable dish, can be quickly microwaved in 3 to 4 minutes on high. Add a little brown sugar and butter to taste. You can also microwave 4 medium sweet potatoes (about 1½ pounds) by piercing with fork in several places to allow steam to escape. Arrange in circle on microwavable paper towel in microwave oven. Microwave uncovered on high 8 to 15 minutes or until tender when pierced with fork. Let stand uncovered 5 minutes.

TIMETABLE

1. Microwave bacon for Spinach Salad.

2. Place ham from Sherried Ham Dijon in dish and brush with sherry mixture.

3. Heat or microwave sweet potatoes.

4. Microwave ham.

5. Prepare salad.

NUTRITION INFORMATION PER SERVING

Calories	510	Percent of U.S. RDA	
Protein, grams	30	Protein	46
Carbohydrate, grams	36	Vitamin A	100
Fat, grams	28	Vitamin C	50
Cholesterol, milligrams	130	Thiamin	78
Sodium, milligrams	1780	Riboflavin	38
Potassium, milligrams	1150	Niacin	40
		Calcium	18
		Iron	30

Menu #59

SHERRIED HAM DIJON

1 fully cooked smoked ham
  slice, about 1 inch thick
  (about 1 pound)
2 tablespoons Dijon mustard
1 tablespoon sherry, dry
  white wine or apple juice
Freshly ground pepper
2 tablespoons mustard seed
Chopped fresh parsley, if
  desired

Slash outer edge of fat on ham slice diagonally at 1-inch intervals to prevent curling. Place ham in rectangular microwavable dish, 11 × 7 × 1½ inches. Mix mustard and sherry; brush over ham. Sprinkle with pepper and mustard seed. Cover with waxed paper and microwave on medium-high (70%) 8 to 10 minutes, rotating dish ½ turn after 4 minutes, until ham is hot. Sprinkle with chopped parsley. Let stand covered about 3 minutes.

SPINACH SALAD

3 slices bacon, cut into 1-inch
  pieces
¾ pound spinach, torn into
  bite-size pieces (about
  6 cups)
3 ounces mushrooms, sliced
  (about 1 cup)
1 small onion, chopped
  (about ¼ cup)
1 teaspoon sugar
¼ teaspoon dry mustard
¼ teaspoon pepper
3 tablespoons cider vinegar
2 tablespoons grated
  Parmesan cheese
1 hard-cooked egg, finely
  chopped

Place bacon in 4-cup microwavable measure. Cover loosely and microwave on high 3 to 4 minutes or until crisp. Remove bacon with slotted spoon; drain. Reserve bacon and fat.

Mix spinach and mushrooms in large bowl. Stir onion into bacon fat in 4-cup measure. Cover loosely and microwave on high about 2 minutes or until soft. Stir in sugar, mustard, pepper and vinegar. Pour over spinach and mushrooms. Toss. Sprinkle with bacon, cheese and egg.

◇
MENU 60

GREEK MINI MEAT LOAVES* • EASY RATATOUILLE* • CREAMY CUCUMBER SALAD • RASPBERRY PEARS*

MENU MAKES 4 SERVINGS

INGREDIENTS

½ cup uncooked instant rice

¼ cup raspberry jam

¼ cup chocolate syrup

1 can (28 ounces) pear halves in juice

1 can (16 ounces) zucchini with Italian-style tomato sauce

2 tablespoons lemon juice

½ teaspoon chopped garlic

1 teaspoon chopped fresh or ½ teaspoon dried basil

2 teaspoons chopped fresh or 1 teaspoon dried mint

½ teaspoon pepper

½ teaspoon salt

½ pound eggplant

1 small onion

1 lemon

1 pound ground lamb or beef

¼ cup sour cream

1 egg

1⅓ cups creamy cucumber salad

MENU TIP: Pick up the creamy cucumber salad at the deli. Also, keep chopped onions on hand in the freezer—see page 3 for freezing directions.

TIMETABLE

1. Prepare Easy Ratatouille.

2. Prepare Greek Mini Meat Loaves.

3. Prepare Raspberry Pears.

NUTRITION INFORMATION PER SERVING

		Percent of U.S. RDA	
Calories	610		
Protein, grams	37	Protein	56
Carbohydrate, grams	83	Vitamin A	24
Fat, grams	16	Vitamin C	20
Cholesterol, milligrams	165	Thiamin	30
Sodium, milligrams	710	Riboflavin	30
Potassium, milligrams	1150	Niacin	44
		Calcium	10
		Iron	30

GREEK MINI MEAT LOAVES

1 pound ground lamb or beef
½ cup uncooked instant rice
1 small onion, chopped
  (about ¼ cup)
1 egg
2 tablespoons lemon juice
2 teaspoons chopped fresh or
  1 teaspoon dried mint
½ teaspoon salt
¼ teaspoon pepper
4 thin lemon slices

Mix all ingredients except lemon slices. Shape into 4 small loaves. Place on microwave rack in microwavable dish. Arrange 1 lemon slice on each loaf. Cover with waxed paper and microwave on high 8 to 10 minutes, rotating dish ½ turn after 5 minutes, until no longer pink. Let stand covered 5 minutes.

EASY RATATOUILLE

½ pound eggplant, cut into
  ½-inch cubes (about
  2 cups)
1 can (16 ounces) zucchini
  with Italian-style to-
  mato sauce
½ teaspoon chopped garlic
1 teaspoon chopped fresh or
  ½ teaspoon dried basil
⅛ teaspoon pepper

Mix all ingredients in 1½-quart microwavable casserole. Cover tightly and microwave on high 5 to 8 minutes, stirring after 4 minutes, until eggplant is tender. Let stand covered 5 minutes.

RASPBERRY PEARS

1 can (28 ounces) pear halves
  in juice, drained
¼ cup raspberry jam
¼ cup chocolate syrup
¼ cup sour cream

Divide pear halves among 4 microwavable dessert dishes. Place 1 tablespoon jam over pears in each dish. Just before serving, microwave uncovered on high 1 to 2 minutes or until warm. Drizzle with syrup and serve with sour cream.

Menu #60 (page 171)

◆ MENU 61 ◆

Jambalaya Peppers* • Zucchini and Corn with Cheese* • Lettuce Wedges with Ranch Dressing • Ice Cream with Hot Fudge Sauce*

MENU MAKES 4 SERVINGS

INGREDIENTS

¾ cup uncooked instant rice

½ cup sugar

1 package (6 ounces) semi-sweet chocolate chips

½ teaspoon vanilla

1 can (17 ounces) whole kernel corn

1 can (8 ounces) Italian-style tomato sauce

1 can (7½ ounces) tiny shrimp

1 can (5.33 ounces) evaporated milk

¼ cup ranch salad dressing

1 teaspoon chili powder

⅛ teaspoon salt

⅛ teaspoon pepper

2 large bell peppers

1 medium zucchini (about ¾ pound)

½ head lettuce

4 ounces fully cooked smoked ham

½ cup shredded Cheddar cheese (2 ounces)

2 teaspoons margarine

1 pint ice cream

MENU TIP: The dovetailing in the timetable is the key to this thirty-minute menu. Look for chopped ham in the deli section and also buy shredded cheese. Nutrition information has been calculated with 2 tablespoons fudge sauce per serving of ice cream.

TIMETABLE

1. Prepare Hot Fudge Sauce.

2. Prepare Jambalaya Peppers.

3. Prepare Zucchini and Corn with Cheese.

4. Prepare lettuce wedges with dressing.

5. Microwave zucchini and corn.

NUTRITION INFORMATION PER SERVING

		Percent of U.S. RDA	
Calories	755		
Protein, grams	30	Protein	46
Carbohydrate, grams	98	Vitamin A	42
Fat, grams	29	Vitamin C	98
Cholesterol, milligrams	135	Thiamin	44
Sodium, milligrams	900	Riboflavin	26
Potassium, milligrams	920	Niacin	22
		Calcium	26
		Iron	34

JAMBALAYA PEPPERS

¾ cup uncooked instant rice
1 can (8 ounces) Italian-
style tomato sauce
⅓ cup water
1 teaspoon chili powder
1 can (7½ ounces) tiny
shrimp, drained
1 cup chopped fully cooked
smoked ham (4 ounces)
2 large bell peppers

Mix rice, tomato sauce, water and chili powder in 1-quart microwavable casserole. Cover tightly and microwave on high 5 minutes. Stir in shrimp and ham.

Cut bell peppers in half lengthwise. Remove seeds and membranes; rinse. Arrange peppers, cut sides up, in circle on 9- or 10-inch microwavable pie plate. Fill each pepper with about 1 cup mixture. Cover tightly and microwave on high 7 to 9 minutes, rotating dish ½ turn after 4 minutes, until filling is hot in center. Let stand covered 5 minutes.

ZUCCHINI AND CORN WITH CHEESE

1 medium zucchini (about
¾ pound), cubed
1 can (17 ounces) whole
kernel corn, drained
⅛ teaspoon salt
⅛ teaspoon pepper
½ cup shredded Cheddar
cheese (2 ounces)

Mix zucchini, corn, salt and pepper in 1-quart microwavable casserole. Cover tightly and microwave on high 5 to 7 minutes, stirring after 2 minutes, until vegetables are hot. Sprinkle with cheese. Let stand covered 1 minute.

HOT FUDGE SAUCE

1 can (5.33 ounces) evaporated milk (⅔ cup)
1 package (6 ounces) semi-
sweet chocolate chips
(1 cup)
½ cup sugar
2 teaspoons margarine
½ teaspoon vanilla

Mix milk, chocolate chips and sugar in 2-cup microwavable measure. Microwave uncovered medium (50%) 4 to 6 minutes, stirring every 2 minutes, until boiling. Add margarine and vanilla. Stir vigorously until margarine is melted and sauce is smooth. Serve warm. Cover and refrigerate remaining sauce. **Makes 1½ cups sauce, 2 tablespoons per serving.**

MENU
62

BEAN AND CHEESE TACOS* • CANTALOUPE OR PINEAPPLE WITH LIME WEDGES • BELL PEPPER SLICES • FRUIT AND NUT BREAD PUDDING*

MENU MAKES 4 SERVINGS

INGREDIENTS

1 cup chunky salsa

½ cup dried fruit bits, dried cranberries, dried cherries or raisins

⅓ cup packed brown sugar

¼ cup chopped nuts

1 can (8 ounces) kidney beans

1 tablespoon chopped fresh or 1 teaspoon dried cilantro

1 clove garlic

¼ cup chopped green onions

2 bell peppers (any color)

1 lime

4 cups cut-up cantaloupe or pineapple

1½ cups milk

1 cup ricotta cheese (8 ounces)

¼ cup grated Parmesan cheese

3 tablespoons margarine or butter

2 eggs

4 slices bread

4 flour tortillas (8 inches in diameter)

MENU TIP: Pick up cut-up fresh fruit at the supermarket, or speed preparation by serving melon or pineapple in chunks with the rind on.

TIMETABLE

1. Prepare Fruit and Nut Bread Pudding.

2. Prepare fruit and lime wedges.

3. Prepare bell pepper slices.

4. Prepare Bean and Cheese Tacos.

NUTRITION INFORMATION PER SERVING

		Percent of U.S. RDA	
Calories	705		
Protein, grams	25	Protein	38
Carbohydrate, grams	98	Vitamin A	88
Fat, grams	26	Vitamin C	100
Cholesterol, milligrams	135	Thiamin	34
Sodium, milligrams	730	Riboflavin	38
Potassium, milligrams	1160	Niacin	16
		Calcium	50
		Iron	34

BEAN AND CHEESE TACOS

1 can (8 ounces) kidney beans, drained and liquid reserved
1 clove garlic, finely chopped
4 flour tortillas (8 inches in diameter)
1 cup ricotta cheese (8 ounces)
¼ cup grated Parmesan cheese
¼ cup chopped green onions (with tops)
1 tablespoon chopped fresh or 1 teaspoon dried cilantro
1 cup chunky salsa

Mash kidney beans and garlic with fork or masher. (Add 1 to 2 tablespoons reserved bean liquid if beans are dry.) Spread about ¼ cup of the bean mixture on half of each tortilla to within ½ inch of edge. Mix cheeses, onions and cilantro. Spread mixture over beans. Fold tortillas over filling.

Place double layer of microwavable paper towels in rectangular microwavable dish, 11 × 7 × 1½ inches. Place tacos with folds to outside edges in dish. Cover with waxed paper and microwave on high 4 to 7 minutes, rotating dish ½ turn after 2 minutes, until hot. Cut into wedges if desired. Serve with salsa.

FRUIT AND NUT BREAD PUDDING

1½ cups milk
3 tablespoons margarine or butter
4 cups soft bread cubes (about 4 slices bread)
½ cup dried fruit bits, dried cranberries, dried cherries or raisins
⅓ cup packed brown sugar
¼ cup chopped nuts
2 eggs, beaten
Whipped cream or sour cream, if desired

Place milk and margarine in 4-cup microwavable measure. Microwave uncovered on high 4 minutes. Meanwhile, spread bread cubes evenly in round microwavable dish, 8 × 1½ inches. Sprinkle with fruit bits, brown sugar and nuts.

Quickly stir eggs into warm milk mixture. Pour over fruit. Elevate dish on inverted microwavable dinner plate in microwave. Microwave uncovered on medium-high (70%) 9 to 12 minutes, rotating dish ½ turn after 5 minutes, until center is almost set (center will set while standing). Serve warm with whipped cream or sour cream. Immediately refrigerate any remaining pudding.

MENU
63

MUSHROOM WELSH RABBIT* • TOMATOES AND CUCUMBERS VINAIGRETTE • UPSIDE-DOWN PLUM CAKES*

MENU MAKES 4 SERVINGS

INGREDIENTS

1 cup variety baking mix

1 cup milk

¼ cup beer or white wine

6 tablespoons packed brown sugar

2 tablespoons all-purpose flour

2 tablespoons vegetable oil

½ teaspoon vanilla

¼ cup vinaigrette salad dressing

½ teaspoon dry mustard

¼ teaspoon pepper

1 pound mushrooms

2 medium tomatoes

1 medium cucumber

4 green onions

4 medium plums

1 cup shredded Cheddar cheese (4 ounces)

Whipped cream or vanilla yogurt, if desired

6 tablespoons margarine or butter

1 egg

4 slices bread

MENU TIP: Buy mushrooms already sliced in the produce section, or load up at a salad bar. You can also buy a marinated salad at a deli or in the deli section of a supermarket.

TIMETABLE

1. Slice tomatoes and cucumber; mix with vinaigrette salad dressing. Cover and refrigerate.

2. Prepare Upside-down Plum Cakes.

3. Prepare Mushroom Welsh Rabbit.

NUTRITION INFORMATION PER SERVING

Calories	835	**Percent of U.S. RDA**	
Protein, grams	20	Protein	30
Carbohydrate, grams	81	Vitamin A	48
Fat, grams	50	Vitamin C	26
Cholesterol, milligrams	85	Thiamin	36
Sodium, milligrams	950	Riboflavin	66
Potassium, milligrams	1060	Niacin	40
		Calcium	40
		Iron	28

Mushroom Welsh Rabbit

*2 tablespoons margarine or
butter*
*2 tablespoons all-purpose
flour*
¼ teaspoon pepper
½ teaspoon dry mustard
½ cup milk
¼ cup beer or white wine★
*1 cup shredded Cheddar
cheese (4 ounces)*
*1 pound mushrooms, sliced
(about 6 cups)*
*¼ cup sliced green onions,
with tops (about
4 onions)*
*1 tablespoon margarine or
butter*
*4 slices toast, cut into
triangles*

Place 2 tablespoons margarine in 4-cup microwavable measure. Microwave uncovered on high 30 to 60 seconds or until melted. Stir in flour, pepper and mustard. Stir in ½ cup milk. Microwave uncovered on high 1 minute 30 seconds to 2 minutes 30 seconds, stirring every minute, until very thick. Gradually stir in beer. Stir in cheese. Microwave uncovered 2 to 3 minutes, stirring every minute, until cheese is melted.

Place mushrooms, onions and 1 tablespoon margarine in 2-quart microwavable casserole. Cover tightly and microwave on high 5 to 6 minutes, stirring after 2 minutes, until mushrooms are tender; drain. Arrange mushrooms over toast. Pour cheese sauce over mushrooms.

★Beer or wine can be omitted. Increase milk to ¾ cup.

Upside-down Plum Cakes

*3 tablespoons packed brown
sugar*
*3 tablespoons margarine or
butter*
*4 medium plums, thinly
sliced*
1 cup variety baking mix
*3 tablespoons packed brown
sugar*
⅓ cup milk
2 tablespoons vegetable oil
½ teaspoon vanilla
1 egg
*Whipped cream or vanilla
yogurt, if desired*

Place 3 tablespoons brown sugar and the margarine in 1-cup microwavable measure. Microwave uncovered on high about 1 minute or until sugar is melted and mixture can be stirred smooth. Divide caramel mixture among four 10-ounce custard cups. Arrange 1 sliced plum, overlapping slices, in bottom of each cup.

Beat remaining ingredients except whipped cream in medium bowl with wire whisk or hand beater until well blended. Divide batter among cups. Arrange cups in circle in microwave oven. Microwave uncovered on high 5 to 6 minutes, rotating cups ½ turn after 2 minutes, until tops are almost dry and toothpick inserted in centers comes out clean. (Center of cakes may appear slightly moist but will continue to cook while standing.) Let cakes stand uncovered on flat heatproof surface (not wire rack) 2 minutes. Loosen edge. Invert cakes onto heatproof serving plates. Serve warm with whipped cream or vanilla yogurt.

Menu #63 (page 179)

◆ MENU 64 ◆

REUBEN POCKETS* ◆ GERMAN POTATO SALAD ◆ CARROT STICKS ◆ APPLE-WALNUT CAKE*

MENU MAKES 4 SERVINGS

INGREDIENTS

1 cup variety baking mix

¾ cup granulated sugar

⅓ cup vegetable oil

¼ cup packed brown sugar

½ teaspoon vanilla

¾ cup chopped walnuts

1 can (8 ounces) sauerkraut

⅓ cup Thousand Island dressing

2 teaspoons caraway seed, if desired

1½ teaspoons ground cinnamon

4 ounces carrot sticks or 2 carrots

3 medium red all-purpose apples

6 ounces thinly sliced corned beef

1 cup shredded Swiss cheese (4 ounces)

Whipped cream or ice cream, if desired

2 eggs

2 pita breads (about 6 inches in diameter)

3 cups German potato salad

MENU TIP: Purchase canned or deli German potato salad, and buy cut-up carrots and chopped nuts, or keep your own homemade supply on hand. The nutrition information has been calculated for 1 serving of cake.

TIMETABLE

1. Prepare and microwave Apple-Walnut Cake.

2. Mix ingredients for Reuben Pockets; fill pockets.

3. Place German potato salad in microwavable bowl. Cover tightly and microwave on high 3 to 5 minutes, stirring after 2 minutes until warm.

4. Microwave pockets.

NUTRITION INFORMATION PER SERVING

		Percent of U.S. RDA	
Calories	975		
Protein, grams	32	Protein	48
Carbohydrate, grams	102	Vitamin A	100
Fat, grams	51	Vitamin C	26
Cholesterol, milligrams	125	Thiamin	22
Sodium, milligrams	1770	Riboflavin	22
Potassium, milligrams	940	Niacin	20
		Calcium	36
		Iron	20

REUBEN POCKETS

6 ounces thinly sliced corned beef, coarsely chopped
1 can (8 ounces) sauerkraut, rinsed and well drained
1 cup shredded Swiss cheese (4 ounces)
⅓ cup Thousand Island dressing
2 teaspoons caraway seed, if desired
2 pita breads (about 6 inches in diameter), cut in half

Mix all ingredients except pita breads in bowl. Fill breads with corned beef mixture. Arrange pita breads in circle on microwavable rack. Cover with microwavable paper towel and microwave on medium (50%) 4 to 5 minutes, rotating dish ½ turn after 2 minutes, until filling is hot and cheese is melted.

APPLE-WALNUT CAKE

1 cup variety baking mix
¾ cup granulated sugar
½ cup coarsely chopped walnuts
2 medium red all-purpose apples, unpared and shredded (about 1½ cups)
⅓ cup vegetable oil
1½ teaspoons ground cinnamon
½ teaspoon vanilla
2 eggs
1 medium red all-purpose apple, unpared and thinly sliced
¼ cup chopped walnuts
¼ cup packed brown sugar
Whipped cream or ice cream, if desired

Lightly grease bottom only of round microwavable dish, 8 × 1½ inches.

Mix baking mix, granulated sugar, ½ cup walnuts, the shredded apple, oil, cinnamon, vanilla and eggs until blended. Beat 1 minute. Pour into dish. Cover dish with waxed paper and elevate on inverted microwavable dinner plate in microwave oven. Microwave on high 5 minutes. (Cake will be partially cooked.)

Arrange apple slices in spoke fashion on cake. Sprinkle evenly with ¼ cup chopped walnuts and the brown sugar. Microwave uncovered 4 to 6 minutes or until apple slices are slightly tender and toothpick inserted in center of cake comes out clean. Let stand uncovered at least 5 minutes. Serve warm or cool with whipped cream or ice cream. **8 portions, 1 per serving.**

SPICY SAUSAGE CHILI* • COUNTRY CORN MUFFINS* • TOSSED SALAD

MENU MAKES 4 SERVINGS

INGREDIENTS

1 cup variety baking mix

¼ cup beer or water

1 can (16 ounces) hot chili beans

1 can (16 ounces) tomatoes

1 can (8 ounces) whole kernel corn

¼ cup blue cheese salad dressing

2 cloves garlic

1 medium onion

2 teaspoons chili powder

1 teaspoon ground cumin

Paprika

1 medium bell pepper

4 cups mixed salad greens

¼ cucumber, sliced

½ pound spicy Italian sausage

1 egg

MENU TIP: A full, robust chili flavor can be achieved in seconds if you start with chili beans packed with chili, rather than plain pinto or kidney beans. The nutrition information has been calculated for 1 muffin per serving.

TIMETABLE

1. Prepare Spicy Sausage Chili.

2. Prepare salad.

3. Prepare Country Corn Muffins.

NUTRITION INFORMATION PER SERVING

Calories	440	**Percent of U.S. RDA**	
Protein, grams	18	Protein	26
Carbohydrate, grams	42	Vitamin A	48
Fat, grams	24	Vitamin C	76
Cholesterol, milligrams	70	Thiamin	24
Sodium, milligrams	1210	Riboflavin	22
Potassium, milligrams	960	Niacin	24
		Calcium	14
		Iron	28

SPICY SAUSAGE CHILI

½ pound spicy Italian
  sausage
1 medium bell pepper,
  chopped
1 medium onion, chopped
  (about ½ cup)
2 cloves garlic, chopped
2 teaspoons chili powder
1 teaspoon ground cumin
1 can (16 ounces) hot chili
  beans
1 can (16 ounces) tomatoes,
  undrained

Place sausage, bell pepper, onion, garlic and chili powder in 2-quart microwavable casserole. Cover tightly and microwave on high 3 to 5 minutes, stirring and breaking up sausage after 2 minutes, until sausage is no longer pink; drain. Stir in remaining ingredients. Cover tightly and microwave 10 to 12 minutes, stirring after 5 minutes, until hot and bubbly.

COUNTRY CORN MUFFINS

1 can (8 ounces) whole kernel corn, drained
¼ cup beer or water
1 egg
1 cup variety baking mix
Paprika

Line 6-cup microwavable muffin ring or 6-ounce custard cups with paper baking cups. Mix corn, beer and egg in small bowl. Stir in baking mix just until moistened. Fill each cup with scant ⅓ cup batter. Sprinkle with paprika. Microwave uncovered on high 2 to 4 minutes, rotating ring ¼ turn every minute, until tops are almost dry and toothpick inserted in centers comes out clean. (Parts of muffins may appear slightly moist but will continue to cook while standing.) Cool 2 minutes before removing muffins from ring. Serve warm. **6 muffins, 1 per serving.**

POACHED CHICKEN WITH VEGETABLES[*] ✦ GARLICKY PARMESAN POTATOES[*] ✦ CRANBERRY SAUCE IN LETTUCE CUPS ✦ CHOCOLATE ICE CREAM WITH COCONUT-PECAN SAUCE[*]

MENU MAKES 4 SERVINGS

INGREDIENTS

1 cup packed brown sugar

½ cup flaked coconut

½ cup chopped pecans

2 tablespoons corn syrup

2 tablespoons dry white wine or chicken broth

1 tablespoon cornstarch

1 cup cranberry sauce

1½ teaspoons chopped fresh or ½ teaspoon dried marjoram

3 gloves garlic

½ teaspoon salt

4 medium potatoes (about 1½ pounds)

1 medium carrot

1 medium leek

1 medium zucchini

4 cupped lettuce leaves

1 lemon

4 skinless boneless chicken breast halves

½ cup half-and-half

½ cup (1 stick) margarine or butter

¼ cup grated Parmesan cheese

2 cups chocolate ice cream

MENU TIP: This is a perfect menu for your food processor. Use it to julienne the vegetables for the chicken and slice the potatoes too. To make lettuce cups, use leaves from the center of the head. The nutrition information has been calculated with 2 tablespoons Coconut-Pecan Sauce per serving of chocolate ice cream.

TIMETABLE

1. Prepare Coconut-Pecan Sauce.

2. Prepare Garlicky Parmesan Potatoes.

3. Prepare Poached Chicken with Vegetables.

4. Place cranberry sauce in lettuce cups.

NUTRITION INFORMATION PER SERVING

Calories	860	**Percent of U.S. RDA**	
Protein, grams	36	Protein	54
Carbohydrate, grams	113	Vitamin A	100
Fat, grams	34	Vitamin C	16
Cholesterol, milligrams	85	Thiamin	18
Sodium, milligrams	750	Riboflavin	26
Potassium, milligrams	1360	Niacin	60
		Calcium	32
		Iron	78

Menu #66 (page 187)

Poached Chicken with Vegetables

4 skinless boneless chicken
   breast halves
½ teaspoon salt
1½ teaspoons chopped fresh
   or ½ teaspoon dried
   marjoram
1 medium carrot, coarsely
   shredded
1 medium leek, thinly sliced
1 medium zucchini, cut into
   thin strips
2 tablespoons margarine or
   butter, melted
2 tablespoons dry white
   wine or chicken broth
4 thin lemon slices

Arrange chicken with thickest parts to outside edges in square microwavable dish, 8 × 8 × 2 inches. Sprinkle with salt and half of the marjoram. Place vegetables over chicken. Drizzle with margarine and wine. Sprinkle with remaining marjoram. Top each with lemon slice. Cover with plastic wrap, folding back one corner. Microwave on high 10 to 12 minutes, rotating dish ½ turn after 5 minutes, until juices of chicken run clear and vegetables are crisp-tender.

Garlicky Parmesan Potatoes

4 medium potatoes (about
   1½ pounds), thinly sliced
2 tablespoons margarine or
   butter, melted
3 cloves garlic, finely
   chopped
¼ cup grated Parmesan
   cheese

Place potato slices in 1½-quart microwavable casserole. Drizzle potatoes with margarine. Sprinkle with garlic and half of the cheese. Cover tightly and microwave on high 4 minutes. Stir and sprinkle with remaining cheese. Cover tightly and microwave 3 to 6 minutes or until potatoes are tender. Let stand covered 3 minutes.

Coconut-Pecan Sauce

1 tablespoon cornstarch
1 cup packed brown sugar
½ cup half-and-half
½ cup flaked coconut
½ cup chopped pecans
¼ cup margarine or butter
2 tablespoons corn syrup

Mix cornstarch and brown sugar in 1½-quart microwavable casserole or 8-cup microwavable measure. Stir in remaining ingredients. Cover tightly and microwave on high 3 to 5 minutes, stirring every minute, until sauce is thickened and sugar is dissolved. Serve warm. Cover and refrigerate remaining sauce. **About 1½ cups sauce, 2 tablespoons per serving.**

◆ MENU 67 ◆

CURRIED CHICKEN CASSEROLE*
◆ CHUTNEY ZUCCHINI* ◆ BREADSTICKS ◆
FRESH FRUIT

MENU MAKES 4 SERVINGS

INGREDIENTS

1 cup uncooked instant rice

⅓ cup raisins

1 teaspoon cornstarch

⅓ cup coarsely chopped dry roasted peanuts

¼ cup chutney

1 can (10½ ounces) condensed cream of chicken soup

2 teaspoons curry powder

½ teaspoon ground cumin

2 medium zucchini

2 medium stalks celery

1 small onion

4 peaches, pears or other fruit

2 cups cut-up cooked chicken or turkey, or 2 cans (5 ounces each) boned chicken, cut up

4 breadsticks

MENU TIP: Dessert can be as simple—and satisfying—as a bowl of fresh fruit for the choosing. If you prefer, purchase cut-up fresh fruit in the produce section or from the salad bar at the supermarket.

TIMETABLE

1. Prepare Curried Chicken Casserole.

2. Prepare Chutney Zucchini.

NUTRITION INFORMATION PER SERVING

		Percent of U.S. RDA	
Calories	675		
Protein, grams	31	Protein	46
Carbohydrate, grams	106	Vitamin A	32
Fat, grams	15	Vitamin C	14
Cholesterol, milligrams	55	Thiamin	30
Sodium, milligrams	710	Riboflavin	14
Potassium, milligrams	990	Niacin	52
		Calcium	8
		Iron	28

CURRIED CHICKEN CASSEROLE

1 can (10½ ounces) con-
    densed cream of chicken
    soup
¾ cup water
2 teaspoons curry powder
½ teaspoon ground cumin
2 cups cut-up cooked chicken
    or turkey, or 2 cans
    (5 ounces each) boned
    chicken, cut up
2 medium stalks celery,
    thinly sliced (about 1 cup)
1 small onion, chopped
    (about ¼ cup)
1 cup uncooked instant rice
⅓ cup raisins
⅓ cup coarsely chopped dry
    roasted peanuts

Mix soup, water, curry powder and cumin in 1½-quart microwavable casserole. Stir in chicken, celery, onion, rice and raisins. Cover tightly and microwave on high 10 to 12 minutes, stirring after 5 minutes, until rice is tender and mixture is hot. Sprinkle with peanuts.

CHUTNEY ZUCCHINI

1 teaspoon cornstarch
¼ cup chutney
2 medium zucchini, cut
    crosswise into thin slices

Stir cornstarch into chutney in 2-quart microwavable casserole. Stir in zucchini. Cover tightly and microwave on high 4 to 6 minutes, stirring after 3 minutes, until zucchini is crisp-tender; stir.

◆ MENU 68 ◆

ORANGE TERIYAKI CHICKEN* ◆ RICE ◆ ORIENTAL SPINACH*

MENU MAKES 4 SERVINGS

INGREDIENTS

⅔ cup uncooked regular long grain or 1 cup uncooked instant rice

2 tablespoons packed brown sugar

1 tablespoon and 2 teaspoons cornstarch

2 tablespoons vegetable oil

1 teaspoon granulated sugar

½ cup dry white or rosé wine or apple juice

1 can (11 ounces) mandarin orange segments

1 can (8 ounces) sliced water chestnuts

½ cup teriyaki sauce

1 tablespoon soy sauce

1¼ teaspoons finely chopped gingerroot or ¾ teaspoon ground ginger

½ teaspoon finely chopped garlic

6 ounces mushrooms

2 green onions

1 small onion

4 skinless boneless chicken breast halves

1 package (10 ounces) frozen leaf spinach

MENU TIP: Preparing the rice conventionally leaves the microwave free for the meat and vegetables and still keeps you on schedule. Buy mushrooms already sliced in the produce section or at the salad bar.

TIMETABLE

1. Prepare rice.

2. Prepare Orange Teriyaki Chicken.

3. Prepare Oriental Spinach.

NUTRITION INFORMATION PER SERVING

		Percent of U.S. RDA	
Calories	525		
Protein, grams	35	Protein	54
Carbohydrate, grams	66	Vitamin A	100
Fat, grams	11	Vitamin C	50
Cholesterol, milligrams	80	Thiamin	38
Sodium, milligrams	2470	Riboflavin	38
Potassium, milligrams	1310	Niacin	68
		Calcium	14
		Iron	28

ORANGE TERIYAKI CHICKEN

4 skinless boneless chicken
  breast halves (about
  1 pound)
1 tablespoon and 2 teaspoons
  cornstarch
2 tablespoons packed brown
  sugar
1 tablespoon vegetable oil
¼ teaspoon finely chopped
  garlic
½ cup dry white or rosé
  wine or apple juice
½ cup teriyaki sauce
2 cups hot cooked rice
1 can (11 ounces) manda-
  rin orange segments,
  drained
2 green onions (with tops),
  thinly sliced

Pierce chicken breast halves with fork. Arrange chicken with thickest parts to outside edge in 3-quart microwavable casserole. Mix cornstarch, brown sugar, vegetable oil, garlic, dry white wine and teriyaki sauce. Pour over chicken. Cover tightly and microwave on high 10 to 12 minutes, spooning sauce over chicken and rotating casse-role ½ turn after 5 minutes, until juices of chicken run clear. Serve chicken over rice. Top with mandarin orange segments and onions.

ORIENTAL SPINACH

1 package (10 ounces) frozen leaf spinach
1 tablespoon vegetable oil
1¼ teaspoons finely chopped
  gingerroot or ¾ teaspoon
  ground ginger
1 small onion, chopped
  (about ¼ cup)
¼ teaspoon finely chopped
  garlic
6 ounces mushrooms, sliced
  (about 2 cups)
1 can (8 ounces) sliced water chestnuts, drained
1 tablespoon soy sauce
1 teaspoon granulated
  sugar

Place spinach in 2-quart microwavable casserole. Cover tightly and microwave on high 4 minutes. Break up spinach; drain well. Stir in remaining ingredients. Cover tightly and microwave on high 2 to 4 minutes longer, until spinach is hot and crisp-tender.

Menu #68 (page 193)

◆ MENU 69 ◆

CHICKEN ENCHILADAS*
◆ FRESH FRUIT SALAD ◆ EGG CUSTARDS*

MENU MAKES 4 SERVINGS

INGREDIENTS

¼ cup sugar

1 teaspoon vanilla

Caramel topping, if desired

Taco sauce, if desired

1 can (4 ounces) chopped green chilies

1 clove garlic

Ground nutmeg

Dash of salt

1 medium onion

1 medium tomato

2 cups cut-up cooked chicken or turkey

1¼ cups milk

1 cup shredded Cheddar cheese (4 ounces)

3 eggs

8 flour tortillas (6 inches in diameter)

1 container (6 ounces) frozen avocado dip

2 cups fresh fruit salad

MENU TIP: Buy fresh fruit salad from a deli or cut-up fresh fruit from a salad bar. Cut-up cooked chicken or turkey is available in some markets, or you can buy a 12-ounce piece of cooked poultry from a deli.

TIMETABLE

1. Prepare Egg Custards.

2. Prepare and microwave four Chicken Enchiladas. Assemble remaining enchiladas while first four are cooking; microwave.

NUTRITION INFORMATION PER SERVING

			Percent of U.S. RDA	
Calories	605			
Protein, grams	35		Protein	54
Carbohydrate, grams	57		Vitamin A	40
Fat, grams	27		Vitamin C	22
Cholesterol, milligrams	245		Thiamin	16
Sodium, milligrams	440		Riboflavin	38
Potassium, milligrams	890		Niacin	28
			Calcium	44
			Iron	22

CHICKEN ENCHILADAS

*2 cups cut-up cooked chicken
or turkey*
*1 can (4 ounces) chopped
green chilies, drained*
*1 medium tomato, chopped
(about ¾ cup)*
*1 medium onion, chopped
(about ½ cup)*
1 clove garlic, finely chopped
*8 flour tortillas (6 inches in
diameter)*
*1 container (6 ounces) fro-
zen avocado dip, thawed*
*1 cup shredded Cheddar
cheese (4 ounces)*
Taco sauce, if desired

Mix chicken, chilies, tomato, onion and garlic in 1½-quart microwavable casserole. Cover tightly and microwave on high 5 to 6 minutes, stirring after 2 minutes, until hot.

Place 4 tortillas on 10-inch microwavable plate. Cover tightly and microwave on high 20 to 30 seconds or until hot. Place about ⅓ cup chicken mixture down center of each tortilla; top each with about 1 tablespoon of the avocado dip.

Roll tortillas around filling. Arrange tortillas, seam sides down, on plate. Sprinkle with ½ cup of the cheese. Microwave uncovered on high 2 to 3 minutes or until enchiladas are hot and cheese is melted. Repeat with remaining tortillas. Serve with taco sauce.

EGG CUSTARDS

1¼ cups milk
3 eggs
¼ cup sugar
1 teaspoon vanilla
Dash of salt
Ground nutmeg
Caramel topping, if desired

Microwave milk uncovered on high 3 to 4 minutes or until hot but not boiling. Beat eggs slightly in 4-cup measure, using wire whisk or hand beater. Beat in sugar, vanilla and salt until slightly foamy and well blended. Gradually beat in hot milk. Pour into four 6-ounce custard cups. Sprinkle with nutmeg. Arrange custard cups on 10-inch plate.

Microwave uncovered on medium (50%) 4 to 6 minutes, rotating plate ½ turn and rearranging custard cups after 2 minutes, just until set. (Tops will appear slightly wet but will set completely during refrigeration.) Refrigerate at least 15 minutes. Unmold to serve. Serve with caramel topping. Immediately refrigerate any remaining custards.

◆ MENU 70 ◆

TURKEY BURGERS* ◆ CHIPOTLE SAUCE* ◆ ORANGE AND JICAMA WITH HONEY AND LIME ◆ ANGEL FOOD CAKE WITH RUM-RAISIN FUDGE SAUCE*

MENU MAKES 4 SERVINGS

INGREDIENTS

1 cup hot fudge sauce

¼ cup raisins

2 tablespoons rum

2 tablespoons honey

2 tablespoons creamy peanut butter

1 chipotle chili in adobo sauce

2 tablespoons lime juice

1 tablespoon Worcestershire sauce

½ teaspoon salt

8 ounces jicama

3 green onions

2 oranges

1 pound ground turkey

½ cup plain yogurt

2 tablespoons milk

4 hamburger buns, if desired

4 slices angel food cake

MENU TIP: Chop the green onions all at once for both the burgers and sauce. You'll find a food processor or salad maker makes quick work of the julienne-cut jicama.

TIMETABLE

1. Microwave rum and raisins for Rum-Raisin Fudge Sauce.

2. Mix Chipotle Sauce.

3. Pare and slice oranges; cut jicama into julienne strips. Drizzle with honey and lime juice.

4. Prepare patties for Turkey Burgers.

5. Microwave fudge sauce.

6. Microwave burgers.

7. Microwave Chipotle Sauce.

NUTRITION INFORMATION PER SERVING

		Percent of U.S. RDA	
Calories	820		
Protein, grams	32	Protein	48
Carbohydrate, grams	134	Vitamin A	16
Fat, grams	18	Vitamin C	52
Cholesterol, milligrams	65	Thiamin	22
Sodium, milligrams	710	Riboflavin	30
Potassium, milligrams	970	Niacin	36
		Calcium	28
		Iron	30

TURKEY BURGERS

1 pound ground turkey
2 green onions, finely
　chopped
1 tablespoon Worcestershire
　sauce
¼ teaspoon salt
4 hamburger buns, split,
　toasted, if desired

Mix all ingredients except buns. Shape mixture into 4 patties, each about ¾ inch thick. Arrange patties on microwavable rack in microwavable dish. Cover with waxed paper and microwave on high 6 to 7 minutes, turning patties over after 3 minutes, until no longer pink in center. Let stand covered 3 minutes. Serve on buns with Chipotle Sauce.

CHIPOTLE SAUCE

½ cup plain yogurt
2 tablespoons chopped green
　onions
1 to 2 tablespoons chopped,
　seeded, drained canned
　chipotle chilies in adobo
　sauce
2 tablespoons creamy pea-
　nut butter
⅛ teaspoon salt

Place all ingredients in blender or food processor. Cover and blend on medium speed or process about 20 seconds or until well blended. Pour sauce into 1-cup microwavable measure. Microwave uncovered on high about 1 minute 30 seconds, stirring every 15 seconds, until hot.

RUM-RAISIN FUDGE SAUCE

¼ cup raisins
2 tablespoons rum or water
1 cup hot fudge sauce
2 tablespoons milk

Place raisins and rum in 2-cup microwavable measure. Microwave uncovered on high 1 minute; stir. Let stand uncovered 5 minutes. Add hot fudge sauce and milk. Microwave uncovered about 1 minute or until hot. Stir. Serve warm.

**MENU
71**

ORANGE-HERBED FISH* • TOMATOES WITH FETA CHEESE* • CHILLED ASPARAGUS WITH FRENCH DRESSING • MEXICAN HOT FUDGE SUNDAE CAKE*

MENU MAKES 4 SERVINGS

INGREDIENTS

½ cup all-purpose flour

½ cup packed brown sugar

⅓ cup granulated sugar

2 tablespoons cocoa

1 tablespoon vegetable oil

1 teaspoon baking powder

½ teaspoon vanilla

½ cup chopped Brazil nuts or pecans

2 tablespoons coffee liqueur

1 tablespoon instant espresso coffee

¼ cup French dressing

2 tablespoons chopped pitted ripe olives

1 can (14 ounces) asparagus spears

2 teaspoons chopped fresh or ½ teaspoon dried basil

1 clove garlic

Salt

Pepper

2 medium tomatoes (about ¾ pound)

1 green onion

1 orange

1 pound orange roughy or sole fillets

¼ cup milk

¼ cup crumbled feta or shredded mozzarella cheese (1 ounce)

2 tablespoons margarine or butter

1 cup cinnamon or vanilla ice cream

MENU TIP: Use canned chopped ripe olives to speed preparation of the tomatoes with Feta Cheese and don't bother to get out the electric mixer—the dessert is easy to mix by hand. You can also chill the asparagus in the refrigerator overnight.

TIMETABLE

1. Place asparagus in the freezer to chill for 15 minutes.

2. Prepare Orange-herbed Fish.

3. Prepare Tomatoes with Feta Cheese.

4. Prepare Mexican Hot Fudge Sundae Cake.

5. Arrange asparagus on salad plates and drizzle with dressing.

NUTRITION INFORMATION PER SERVING

		Percent of U.S. RDA	
Calories	800		
Protein, grams	29	Protein	44
Carbohydrate, grams	83	Vitamin A	30
Fat, grams	38	Vitamin C	18
Cholesterol, milligrams	85	Thiamin	20
Sodium, milligrams	910	Riboflavin	16
Potassium, milligrams	1140	Niacin	8
		Calcium	22

ORANGE-HERBED FISH

1 pound orange roughy or
sole fillets
2 tablespoons margarine
or butter, melted
2 teaspoons chopped fresh or
½ teaspoon dried basil
½ teaspoon grated orange
peel
1 clove garlic, finely chopped
2 tablespoons orange juice

Arrange fish with thickest parts to outside edges in rectangular microwavable dish, 11 × 7 × 1½ inches. Brush with margarine. Mix basil, orange peel and garlic. Sprinkle over fish. Drizzle with orange juice. Cover with plastic wrap, folding back one corner. Microwave on high 6 to 8 minutes, rotating dish ½ turn after 3 minutes, until fish flakes easily with fork. Let stand covered 3 minutes.

TOMATOES WITH FETA CHEESE

2 medium tomatoes
Salt and pepper
¼ cup crumbled feta or
shredded mozzarella
cheese (1 ounce)
2 tablespoons chopped pitted ripe olives
1 chopped green onion

Remove stem ends from tomatoes. Cut tomatoes into halves. Arrange cut sides up in circle in microwavable pie plate, 10 × 1½ inches, or on dinner plate. Season with salt and pepper. Cover with waxed paper and microwave on high 2 minutes; rotate pie plate ½ turn. Mix remaining ingredients; sprinkle over tomatoes. Cover and microwave about 2 minutes longer or until tomatoes are hot and cheese is melted.

MEXICAN HOT FUDGE SUNDAE CAKE

½ cup all-purpose flour
⅓ cup granulated sugar
1 tablespoon instant espresso
coffee (dry)
1 teaspoon baking powder
⅛ teaspoon salt
¼ cup milk
1 tablespoon vegetable oil
½ teaspoon vanilla
½ cup chopped pecans
½ cup packed brown sugar
2 tablespoons cocoa
¾ cup very hot water
2 tablespoons coffee liqueur
or hot water
1 cup cinnamon ice cream★

Mix flour, granulated sugar, espresso, baking powder and salt in 1½-quart microwavable casserole or round microwavable dish, 8 × 1½ or 9 × 2 inches. Mix in milk, oil and vanilla with fork until smooth. Stir in nuts. Sprinkle with brown sugar and cocoa. Mix hot water and coffee liqueur. Pour over batter.

Microwave uncovered on medium (50%) 5 minutes; rotate casserole ¼ turn. Microwave uncovered on high 3 to 5 minutes longer or until top is almost dry. Spoon warm cake into dessert dishes and top with ice cream. Spoon sauce from pan onto each serving.

★Vanilla ice cream sprinkled with cinnamon can be substituted for cinnamon ice cream.

PARMESAN SOLE WITH MUSHROOMS* • PASTA • MARINATED VEGETABLE SALAD • BRANDIED NECTARINES AND DATES*

MENU MAKES 4 SERVINGS

INGREDIENTS

½ cup chopped pitted dates or prunes

¼ cup slivered almonds, if desired

¼ cup packed brown sugar

2 tablespoons dry bread crumbs

2 tablespoons brandy or 2 teaspoons brandy extract

1 tablespoon lemon juice

8 ounces uncooked long pasta

½ teaspoon salt

⅛ teaspoon pepper

Paprika

4 ounces mushrooms

1 small onion

Parsley

4 medium nectarines, peaches or apples

1 pound sole fillets

½ cup sour cream

3 tablespoons margarine or butter

3 tablespoons grated Parmesan cheese

Cream, sour cream or yogurt, if desired

2 cups marinated vegetable salad

MENU TIP: Neither the apples nor the nectarines need to be peeled for this dessert, so it comes together quickly. You can rub the blades of a kitchen scissors with vegetable oil or dip in water to cut the dates or prunes in half easily and without sticking.

TIMETABLE

1. Toast almonds if desired.

2. Heat water to boiling for cooking pasta conventionally.

3. Prepare Brandied Nectarines and Dates.

4. Prepare Parmesan Sole with Mushrooms.

5. Cook pasta.

NUTRITION INFORMATION PER SERVING

Calories	780	**Percent of U.S. RDA**	
Protein, grams	35	Protein	52
Carbohydrate, grams	92	Vitamin A	62
Fat, grams	31	Vitamin C	90
Cholesterol, milligrams	120	Thiamin	40
Sodium, milligrams	820	Riboflavin	36
Potassium, milligrams	1700	Niacin	30
		Calcium	16
		Iron	28

PARMESAN SOLE WITH MUSHROOMS

4 ounces mushrooms, sliced
(about 2 cups)
1 small onion, chopped
(about ¼ cup)
1 tablespoon margarine or
butter
1 pound sole fillets
½ teaspoon salt
⅛ teaspoon pepper
½ cup sour cream
3 tablespoons grated
Parmesan cheese
2 tablespoons dry bread
crumbs
Paprika
Snipped fresh parsley

Place mushrooms, onion and margarine in 1-quart microwavable casserole. Cover tightly and microwave on high about 2 minutes or until onion is crisp-tender; stir.

If fish fillets are large, cut into 4 serving pieces. Pat dry. Arrange fish with thickest parts to outside edges in rectangular microwavable dish, 11 × 7 × 1½ inches.

Spoon mushroom mixture over fish and sprinkle with salt and pepper. Cover with waxed paper and microwave on high 3 minutes. Mix sour cream and cheese; spread over mushroom mixture. Sprinkle with bread crumbs. Microwave uncovered 3 to 5 minutes or until fish flakes easily with fork. Sprinkle with paprika and parsley. Serve over pasta if desired.

BRANDIED NECTARINES AND DATES

4 medium nectarines, peaches
or apples, thinly sliced
½ cup chopped pitted dates
or prunes
2 tablespoons margarine or
butter
¼ cup packed brown sugar
1 tablespoon lemon juice
2 tablespoons brandy or 2
teaspoons brandy extract
¼ cup slivered almonds,
toasted if desired
Cream, sour cream or
yogurt, if desired

Mix all ingredients except brandy and almonds in 2-quart microwavable casserole. Microwave uncovered on high 6 to 8 minutes, stirring every 3 minutes, until nectarines are almost tender. Stir in brandy and almonds. Cover with waxed paper and let stand 15 minutes. Serve with cream, sour cream or yogurt.

CRUNCHY PECAN FILLETS* • POTATO SALAD • COLESLAW • BLACK FOREST CRUMBLE*

MENU MAKES 4 SERVINGS

INGREDIENTS

¾ cup ground pecans
(2.5 ounces)

½ cup semisweet chocolate
chips

¼ cup unseasoned dry bread
crumbs

15 crème-filled chocolate
sandwich cookies

1 can (21 ounces) cherry
pie filling

1 can (about 16 ounces) pitted dark sweet cherries

1 teaspoon chopped fresh or
¼ teaspoon crushed dried
rosemary

½ teaspoon salt

1 lemon

1 pound grouper or sole
fillets

1 tablespoon margarine or
butter

2 eggs

Ice cream or whipped
cream, if desired

2 cups coleslaw

2 cups potato salad

MENU TIP: Picking up potato salad and coleslaw at your favorite deli allows enough time to prepare the fish and dessert. The nutrition information has been calculated with 1 serving of crumble.

TIMETABLE

1. Prepare Black Forest Crumble.

2. Prepare Crunchy Pecan Fillets.

NUTRITION INFORMATION PER SERVING

		Percent of U.S. RDA	
Calories	770		
Protein, grams	30	Protein	46
Carbohydrate, grams	72	Vitamin A	22
Fat, grams	41	Vitamin C	26
Cholesterol, milligrams	135	Thiamin	22
Sodium, milligrams	1060	Riboflavin	14
Potassium, milligrams	1140	Niacin	10
		Calcium	6
		Iron	16

CRUNCHY PECAN FILLETS

1 tablespoon margarine or
  butter
2 egg whites
¾ cup ground pecans
¼ cup unseasoned dry bread
  crumbs
1 teaspoon chopped fresh or
  ¼ teaspoon crushed dried
  rosemary
½ teaspoon salt
1 pound grouper or sole fillets
4 lemon wedges

Place margarine on microwavable 12-inch plate or oval platter. Microwave uncovered on high 20 to 45 seconds or until melted. Spread evenly over plate. Beat egg whites with wire whisk or fork until foamy. Mix ground pecans, bread crumbs, rosemary and salt.

If fish fillets are large, cut into 4 serving pieces. Pat dry. Dip fish into egg whites; coat with pecan mixture. Arrange fish with thickest parts to outside edge in single layer on plate. Cover with waxed paper and microwave on high 6 to 8 minutes, turning fish over after 4 minutes, until fish flakes easily with fork. Serve with lemon wedges.

BLACK FOREST CRUMBLE

1 can (21 ounces) cherry pie
  filling
1 can (about 16 ounces) pitted dark sweet cherries,
  drained
2 cups coarsely chopped
  crème-filled chocolate
  sandwich cookies (about
  15 cookies)
½ cup semisweet chocolate
  chips
Ice cream or whipped cream,
  if desired

Mix pie filling and cherries in ungreased square microwavable dish, 8 × 8 × 2 inches. Sprinkle with cookies, then chocolate chips. Microwave uncovered on high 7 to 10 minutes or until fruit is hot and bubbly. Let stand uncovered 10 to 30 minutes. Serve with ice cream or whipped cream. **8 portions, 1 per serving.**

CANADIAN METRIC CONVERSION TABLES

Dry and Liquid Measurements			Temperatures			
IMPERIAL	METRIC		FAHRENHEIT	CELSIUS		
¼ teaspoon	1 mL		32°F	0°C		
½ teaspoon	2 mL		212°F	100°C		
1 teaspoon	5 mL		250°F	121°C		
1 tablespoon	15 mL		275°F	140°C		
2 tablespoons	25 mL		300°F	150°C		
3 tablespoons	50 mL		325°F	160°C		
¼ cup	50 mL		350°F	180°C		
⅓ cup	75 mL		375°F	190°C		
½ cup	125 mL		400°F	200°C		
⅔ cup	150 mL		425°F	220°C		
¾ cup	175 mL		450°F	230°C		
1 cup	250 mL		475°F	240°C		

Common Cooking & Baking Utensil Equivalents

BAKEWARE	IMPERIAL	METRIC
Round Pan	8 × 1½ inches	20 × 4 cm
	9 × 1½ inches	22 × 4 cm
Square Pan	8 × 8 × 2 inches	22 × 22 × 5 cm
	9 × 9 × 2 inches	23 × 23 × 5 cm
Baking Dishes	11 × 7 × 1½ inches	28 × 18 × 4 cm
	12 × 7½ × 2 inches	30 × 19 × 5 cm
	13 × 9 × 2 inches	33 × 23 × 5 cm
Loaf Pan	8½ × 4½ × 2½ inches	22 × 11 × 6 cm
	9 × 5 × 3 inches	23 × 13 × 8 cm
Tube Pan	10 × 4 inches	25 × 10 cm
Jelly Roll Pan	15½ × 10½ × 1 inch	39 × 27 × 2.5 cm
Pie Plate	9 × 1¼ inches	23 × 3.2 cm
	10 × 1½ inches	25 × 4 cm
Muffin Cups	2½ × 1¼ inches	6 × 3.2 cm
	3 × 1½ inches	8 × 4 cm
Skillet	10 inches	25 cm
Casseroles and Saucepans	1 quart	1 L
	1½ quarts	1.5 L
	2 quarts	2 L
	2½ quarts	2.5 L
	3 quarts	3 L
	4 quarts	4 L

Note: The recipes in this cookbook have not been developed or tested in Canadian metric measures. When converting to Canadian metric, some variations in recipe quality may be noted.

INDEX

CREDITS

PRENTICE HALL

Publisher: Nina D. Hoffman
Executive Editor: Rebecca W. Atwater
Editor: Anne Ficklen
Assistant Editor: Rachel Simon
Assistant Art Director: Frederick J. Latasa
Photographic Director: Carmen Bonilla
Senior Production Manager: Susan Joseph
Assistant Managing Editor: Kimberly Ann Ebert

GENERAL MILLS, INC.

Senior Editor: Karen Couné
Recipe Development: Mary H. Johnson, Jean E. Kozar, Linel Reiber
Nutrition Department Consultant: Nancy Holmes, R.D.
Recipe Copy Editor: Deb Hance
Editorial Assistant: Elaine Mitchell
Food Stylists: Kate Courtney, Cindy Lund
Photographer: Nanci Doonan Dixon
Photography Assistants: Val Bourassa, Scott Wyberg
Director, Betty Crocker Food and Publications Center: Marcia Copeland
Assistant Manager, Publications: Lois Tlusty